SPANISH RESOURCES

&ACTIVITIES

for club, class and extracurricular activities

Minerva Figueroa

National Textbook Company
a division of NTC *Publishing Group* • Lincolnwood, Illinois USA

1995 Printing

Published by National Textbook Company, a division of NTC Publishing Group.
© 1986 by NTC Publishing Group, 4255 West Touhy Avenue,
Lincolnwood (Chicago), Illinois 60646-1975 U.S.A.
5 6 7 8 9 ML 9 8 7 6 5 4

Contents

of St. Francis of Assisi; 13. Columbus Day; 14. All Saints' Day and All Souls' Day; 15. December.

Introduction

Every Spanish-language program should offer opportunities outside the classroom to learn more about the Spanish language and Hispanic culture. The best way to achieve this is by establishing an organization that encourages the use of the Spanish language in a congenial atmosphere: the Spanish Club. Through the Spanish Club, enriching learning experiences will be gained through the social interaction of those students most interested in Spanish as a first or second language. The club could be a challenge for students who study Spanish as their second language; they will be encouraged to travel, if only through their readings throughout the Spanish-speaking world, sharing their experiences and interests as they do so. Those who speak Spanish as a first language can make valuable linguistic and cultural contributions to the group. This book will serve as a guide for the leaders and members of the club. There are numerous suggestions for activities that not only encourage the use of the language, but will also stimulate interest in Hispanic peoples and customs even among nonmembers. These activities have been carefully selected to ensure participation by students at all levels of language proficiency. Because these activities take place outside the classroom, there is no academic pressure on the students. Their own spontaneous interest in these activities, which include a fair, pen pals, festivals, costumes, games, and food, will encourage them to participate enthusiastically.

Members will learn how to organize the club, how to conduct formal meetings, and how to select projects. Ideas for games, sports, and parties, as well as recipes for Hispanic dishes are included. Although directed primarily at the high school level, the information and suggestions contained herein will also prove useful to college students and members of other organizations who wish to pursue Spanish language studies.

1

Organizing the Club

1. Benefits of a Spanish Club

For students who are enrolled in a Spanish class, the club can reinforce language studies. It will also provide time for students who share similar interests to get together in a relaxed environment. By presenting new and different kinds of Spanish-related activities to the school, other students will be motivated to enroll in Spanish classes and become active members of the club.

2. Adviser's Role

The adviser has an important role in the success of the club. He or she has to be sure that the club officers and committees are keeping up with their responsibilities. The adviser must show enthusiasm and support for the club's activities, foresee problems that could jeopardize the club, and ultimately help to find solutions to such problems. He or she must attend club meetings, suggest improvements, and help students plan, organize, and implement their club activities while not assuming responsibility for these projects; the responsibility lies with all the members. The role is only that of an adviser, leaving the creativity, enthusiasm, and planning to the members of the club while providing constant support. Some of the adviser's responsibilities are as follows:

- Help develop the club.
- Help recruit members into the club.
- Coordinate the work of the club members.
- Delegate responsibilities and tasks to club members.
- Serve as a liaison between club members and staff administration.
- Guide the group towards its goals.
- Lead the group until new leaders are selected.

3. Use of Spanish

The use of Spanish should be limited to part of each meeting or activity; often a reduction in membership has been the result of conducting the meetings entirely in a foreign language. One of the goals of the Spanish Club is for the members to be able to learn or practice Spanish in a relaxed atmosphere, without the pressure and competition found in the class-room. Therefore, it is important that no one feels self-conscious at meetings. At the same time it is necessary to use Spanish at some point; many activities can be incorporated to accomplish this goal. The games presented in Chapter 6 provide an ideal approach.

4. Membership

It would be ideal to open membership to all those interested. However, physical limitations of the facilities may prevent this. If this is the case, the following requirements could be considered:

- Students with a minimum average of B in Spanish.
- Students who have completed one year of Spanish.
- Students interested in visiting Spanish-speaking countries.
- Native Spanish-speaking students who may or may not be enrolled in Spanish classes.

Some clubs have also required candidates for membership to complete certain assignments before acceptance to make sure that the future members have sufficient interest in the club. They may require candidates to present a paper describing why they want to be members and what expectations they have of the club. For social clubs the only requirements might be the interest in becoming an active member and a membership fee. Each club must establish its own requirements according to individual circumstances.

5. Organization

The organization of the club should start during the first meeting in an informal session. This is an excellent opportunity for members to introduce themselves, giving personal data such as name, address, grade in school, future plans, and what they can offer to the club. This will be a good way to "break the ice" and create a relaxed atmosphere. A discussion should follow to establish the purpose of the club, the benefits the school or community will receive, and what benefits the members will receive.

Other topics open to discussion will be:

- Requirements for membership.
- The club's constitution. (Chapter 2 has sample constitutions.)
- Ideas for the name of the club. (See part 9 of Chapter 1.)
- Arrangements for the first formal meeting.

This informal meeting will be a brainstorming session to establish the groundwork for the club.

6. Committees

In order to successfully organize the club, the chairperson should begin to organize members into committees. This should be done during the first formal meeting. Committee work is usually the opportunity for members who want to be active participants. It is also an excellent training ground for future leadership roles. In these committees, only a few people are involved in planning and organizing specific activities. The committees report their activities and findings to the club members. If the rest of the members agree with a particular activity, the corresponding committee makes the arrangements for it, and all the club members participate and benefit from it. The following are some committees the club could consider:

- *Executive Council:* Includes the president, vice president, secretary, and treasurer. It could be extended to name a second and third vice president and a reporter. Some fluency in Spanish should be attained by these members.
- *Program Committee:* Is responsible for helping the club implement the activities required; involving all members in the activities of the club; and involving the club members in planning, organizing, taking on responsibility, and executing tasks.
- *Planning Committee:* Is responsible for compiling a list of possible activities.
- *Special Committees:* Are appointed by the president on a temporary basis to take care of special interests arising in the group. These committees may be in charge of decorations, publicity for special events, refreshments, etc.

- *Standing Committees:* The members of these committees are appointed by the president or by the appointed or elected chair of each committee. Standing committees have a continuing responsibility in the year-round operation of the club.
- *Other Committees:* Editorial Committee, Library committee, Publicity Committee.

7. Meetings

The meetings should be as interesting and stimulating as possible. During the meetings the planning committee should compile a list of possible activities for approval. Depending on the report, the calendar year for the club will be prepared.

The meetings could have two sessions: business and social. The business-related session could be on future activities, discussion sessions on problems affecting the school, the community, the Spanish Club, or any crisis that the Spanish-speaking countries are facing at that moment. The discussions should take place in a friendly atmosphere with members brought together in a roundtable arrangement, if possible. The social session will be informal: games, films, slides, songs, preparing posters and other materials for special activities, visits to the Spanish class, etc. Members should be notified in advance about each meeting and given any information which will help them participate actively. Those responsible for planning should make every effort to make meetings interesting and rewarding to members. Meetings should begin promptly at the announced time and not run beyond closing time. If there is to be a speaker, he or she should be informed in advance of the time allotted and keep to that time. Meetings planned with the aim of obtaining the greatest membership participation are likely to be well attended and members will want to come again. At every meeting the following should be noted:

- A representative from each committee reports on his or her committee's work.
- A representative from each committee meets with the adviser to discuss problems, ideas, activities, etc., regarding the group.
- A member from each committee will write up a brief report on work in progress: ideas, activities, findings, problems, etc.

8. Time and Place

The meetings should be held at a convenient time and place for all the members. The time should be selected in a way that the meeting will not be interrupted. For example, if the meeting is held during a class period, there should be enough time to cover the entire agenda; otherwise, the meeting has to end suddenly. The best time is usually after school or in the evening. If the meeting is held shortly after school, the best place to hold it is in a classroom or any other room available in the school (gymnasium, cafeteria, or auditorium), taking into consideration the size of the group and the activity for that particular day. Evenings present a good opportunity to hold the meeting at a student's home, if allowed by the parents and the school.

9. Decor

The room where the club members meet regularly should have a Hispanic atmosphere. The room should have posters of different Spanish-speaking countries—Mexico, Spain, Puerto Rico, Venezuela, Guatemala, etc.—representing scenic or important places (landscapes, museums, castles, churches, statues, etc.). The flag of each Spanish-speaking country could be displayed in the room. If authentic flags are not available, some of the students could cut out flags from cardboard and later paint them according to each nation's colors. Some of these posters and decorations can be requested from travel or tourism agencies. Objects such as *piñatas,* ceramics, and souvenirs can be found in local stores. A small library could be set up in one corner of the room with magazines, books, and newspapers. The school's librarian will probably know where to send for subscriptions. A bulletin board should also be available to be used in different ways; for example, to announce a special day or celebration with colorful decorations, photos of past activities, and necessary information. The decor of the room could be an excellent project for the Decoration Committee.

10. Club Name

The name of a club reflects the atmosphere, objectives, and personality of its members. Selecting a name could be a challenge and fun at the same time. The following are a few suggestions:

Don Quijote	Cervantes
La amistad	La patria
El coquí	Español
Hispanoamericano	Latino
Los amigos	La posada
Los taínos	El conquistador

Los aztecas	La borincana
La amistad española	Criollo
Los indios	La mesada
La piñata	La tertulia
El morro	La nación
Los artesanos	Los álamos

11. Club Motto

A few suggestions for the club's motto follow.

1. *Haz bien y no mires a quien.* Do good without looking for credit.
2. *En la unión está la fuerza.* In union there is strength.
3. *Quien adelante no mira detrás se queda.* He who doesn't look forward will end up behind.
4. *Lo que hoy se pierde se gana mañana.* What today is lost will be gained tomorrow.
5. *Quien a un buen árbol se arrima buena sombra lo cobija.* He who comes close to a good tree will be sheltered by good shade.
6. *Cuanto más trabajemos más tenemos.* The harder we work, the more we'll have.
7. *Adelante, siempre adelante.* Forward, always forward.
8. *Sabiduría es mejor que el oro y el dinero.* Wisdom is better than money and gold.
9. *No dejes para mañana lo que puedas hacer hoy.* Never put off until tomorrow what you can do today.
10. *El trabajo ennoblece.* Work ennobles.

12. Colors, Pins, Emblems

Any organization, club, or group needs some kind of identification. The club should consider adopting colors, emblems, and a flag. One suggestion could be to study all the colors of the flags from the Spanish-speaking countries, then to use two or three of the most traditional colors. For an emblem, a flower, a bird, or a famous character could be considered. Once the emblem and colors are chosen, the group should decide if there will be pins, patches, stationery, etc. Because there must be harmony among the emblem, colors, song, and motto and later between the name and the objectives of the club, it is advisable to decide on these during a single session. It would be a good activity to have different committees work on each of these ideas and then present them for adoption.

13. Club Calendar

The group should have two lists of possible activities for the upcoming year. One will include the top ten activities that the group has selected in order of priority; the other should be a list of alternative activities in case the original ones need to be revised. The school calendar should be considered to avoid scheduling activities for the same day as school special events. After a calendar has been decided, each club member should have a copy. One copy should be posted on the club's bulletin board, and an announcement in the school's newspaper would keep the rest of the school body informed.

14. Traditions

Fund-raising and social activities could be considered traditional for a group, club, or organization. Three or four fund-raising activities should be in the club calendar for the year. These activities could include the presentation of a film, a bake sale, a car wash, or a dance. A combination of efforts from two clubs for these activities seems to work very well; for example, a music club and the Spanish Club could offer a Spanish concert, or a home economics class and the Spanish Club could make Hispanic baked goods for a bake sale. This could also be a good opportunity for club recognition.

Traditional social activities are: Hispanic festivals, an annual dance, an annual picnic, an exhibition of the work done by the club, a banquet offering Hispanic food, a Christmas party with Hispanic traditions or dedicated to a specific Spanish-speaking country. Some business-related traditional activities are the initiation of the members and an annual meeting.

15. Initiation

Initiation for new club members should be done a few times during the school year. The date will be scheduled in conjunction with other activities of the club. This way, each new member will have time to get acquainted with the club handbook and to learn or memorize the club motto and pledge. If a new member becomes part of the club close to the initition date, the next date in the schedule will be selected for his or her initiation. An initiation committee should be formed to prepare new members for initiation into the club. One possible initiation program could consist of the following:

1. The initiate will read his or her autobiography in Spanish (no more than two minutes).
2. The initiate will read a poem or a short story, sing a song, or present a skit in Spanish. This can last ten minutes, and should be prepared and rehearsed under the supervision of the initiation committee.
3. Finally, the initiate will recite the club's pledge.
4. The initiate will receive a membership card and the club pin.

All members will welcome the new member(s). The initiation ceremony should take about twenty minutes. After the ceremony refreshments can be served.

16. Handbook

The best proof of the success (or failure) of a club is the handbook. It reflects a record of changes that the club goes through as it grows. A handbook is a constant reference for the members. It will include the following:

- A summary of the purpose of the club.
- The club's colors, motto, emblem, pledge, and objectives.
- Requirements for membership and initiation.
- The committees and their responsibilities.
- The club's bylaws.
- Procedures for conducting meetings.
- Rules for nomination and election of the club's officers, and description of their duties and responsibilities.
- A section with the members' names, addresses, and phone numbers, plus any other important information, including the officers' names, and space available to add the names of new members.

17. Credit Points

Credit for club work will be a good motivation for the members. The club will decide how this will be done. For example, credit may be given for perfect attendance at meetings, participation in club activities, a group project, initiative and originality on special projects (some ideas for projects are presented in Chapter 3), leadership, and cooperation. The club could take advantage of National Hispanic Week during which different individual and group exhibits are presented. Prizes for first, second, and third places, and honorable mention may be awarded. Each prize carries a certain number of points. At the end of the year prizes can be awarded according to the number of points obtained. Prizes such as subscription to a Spanish-language magazine, a bilingual dictionary, a ticket to a Hispanic concert or movie, or a gift certificate for goods at a Hispanic store may be awarded.

2

Parliamentary Procedure

1. Bylaws

In forming an organization there are certain orderly steps to follow for a lasting and strong structure. These orderly steps are called the *bylaws* or *constitution*. Some confusion in the use of these two terms always exists; *bylaws* refers to a body of rules which governs an organization; *constitution* is used in reference to the governing rules of a political institution such as the Constitution of the United States. For the purpose of this book the word *bylaws* is used.

Writing the Bylaws

Since bylaws are followed by members and officers, they should be simple and clearly written. Once they are written and adopted, changes may be made through amendments. A procedure for making changes should be established as part of the bylaws themselves.

Amending the Bylaws

In creating a procedure for amending the bylaws, the committee needs to keep in mind that only club members have the authority to make changes. Members must be notified in advance and in writing of any changes under consideration for amendments. The amendments can be adopted by a two-thirds majority of the members present at the time of the vote.

Reglamentos (Modelos)

Reglamentos del Club de Español

Artículo I. Nombre del club
    Sección 1. El nombre del club es _____.

Artículo II. Objetivos
    Sección 1. Para un enriquecimiento constante del idioma.

    *Sección 2. Para la interacción cultural y lingüística de los miembros con
    personas del habla española.*

Artículo III. Miembros
    Sección 1. Miembros—Elegibilidad (requisitos de membresía)

    Sección 2. Clases de membresía

    Activos—*Estudiantes que demuestren interés en los objetivos del club y que
    deseen hacer contribuciones.*

    Honorarios—*Maestros, padres o individuos distinguidos que sean
    seleccionados por los miembros.*

Artículo IV. Oficiales
    Sección 1. Los oficiales del club son:
        a. Presidente
        b. Vicepresidente
        c. Segundo vicepresidente
        d. Tercer vicepresidente
        e. Secretario(a)
        f. Tesorero(a)
        g. Reportero(a)

    Sección 2. Las responsabilidades de los oficiales son:

        a. Presidente
        *El presidente conduce todas las reuniones del club; mantiene una agenda
        y procede de una manera formal; nombra a los directores y miembros de*

Sample Bylaws

The sample bylaws that follow are intended only as a guide. Bylaws must be sensitive and serve each organization's needs and goals. It is the responsibility of the bylaws committee to make sure they do so.

Bylaws of the Spanish Club

Article I. Club Name
  Section 1. The name of the Club is _____.

Article II. Goals
  Section 1. To achieve a constant enrichment of the language.

  Section 2. To have members interact with the Spanish language and Hispanic people and culture.

Article III. Membership
  Section 1. Members—Eligibility (requirements for membership)

  Section 2. Types of membership

  Active members—Students who demonstrate their interest in the goals of the club and are willing to make positive contributions.

  Honorary members—Teachers, parents, or a distinguished personality selected by the members.

Article IV. Officers
  Section 1. The officers of the club are:
    a. President
    b. Vice President
    c. Second Vice President
    d. Third Vice President
    e. Secretary
    f. Treasurer
    g. Reporter

  Section 2. The duties of the officers are:

    a. President
    The president chairs all club meetings. Has an agenda for each meeting and proceeds in a businesslike manner.

los comités; mantiene una lista de los comités en la mesa mientras preside; evita entrar en las discusiones de las asambleas, pero si es esencial que el presidente se vea envuelto, el vicepresidente debe presidir las reuniones y al presidente no se le debe permitir volver a su cargo hasta después de las votaciones sobre la discusión; cuando es el momento de comenzar la reunión el presidente observa si hay quórum; si es así, declara abierta la sesión.

b. Vicepresidente
El vicepresidente actúa como presidente cuando es necesario. En caso de renuncia del presidente, el vicepresidente toma el lugar de éste. En reuniones oficiales, cuando el presidente esté ausente o cuando la silla esté vacante temporalmente el vicepresidente debe presidir. La oficina del vicepresidente queda vacante cuando el vicepresidente asume la oficina del presidente.

c. Segundo vicepresidente
Es quien preside el comité de Reglamentos.

d. Tercer vicepresidente
Es quien preside el comité de Programas.

e. Secretario(a)
Debe encargarse de las llamadas y los mensajes relacionados con las reuniones; escribir los mensajes según el comité ejecutivo lo estipule; mantener notas de todos los asuntos que se hagan durante la reunión, escribiendo las palabras exactas de las mociones y si las mismas fueron rechazadas o aprobadas; mantener un compendio de las conferencias, si es importante debe grabarla sin hacer comentarios de la misma; mandar invitaciones y notas de agradecimiento a los nuevos miembros, pésames, felicitaciones, etc., a menos que esto sea responsabilidad del comité especial.

Appoints committee chairpersons and committee
members. Keeps a list of committees on the table while
presiding. Refrains from entering the debate of questions
before the assembly; if it is essential that this be done, the
vice president should preside the meeting and the
president not permitted to resume the chair until after the
vote has been taken on the question under discussion.
When the time for the meeting arrives, the president notes
whether a quorum is present; if so, he or she calls the
meeting to order and declares a "quorum is present."

b. Vice President
The vice president acts in place of the president, whenever
needed. In case of resignation of the president, the vice
president automatically becomes the president. In official
meetings, the vice president should preside in the absence
of the president or whenever the president temporarily
vacates the chair. The office of vice president becomes
vacant when the vice president assumes the office of
president.

c. Second Vice President
The second vice president is the chairperson of the Bylaws
Committee.

d. Third Vice President
The third vice president is the chairperson of the Program
Committee.

e. Secretary
The secretary should issue all calls or notices of meetings
and write such letters as the Executive Council may
designate. Keeps a neat and careful record of all business
conducted during the meetings with the exact wording of
every motion and whether it was defeated or carried. Brief
extracts from speeches, if important, may be recorded but
no comments of any kind will be made. The secretary sends
out invitations to new members and notes of thanks,
condolences, congratulations, etc., unless the latter are
associated with the activities of a standing or special
committee.

f. Tesorero(a)
Cobra las cuotas, distribuye las tarjetas de miembros;
mantiene notas de todas las transacciones de negocios;
mantiene un registro de los gastos incurridos por los
miembros o comités; mensualmente declara un estado
financiero y reporta una vez al año o en el momento que el
comité ejecutivo lo solicite. El club debe autorizar la forma
por la cual las facturas deben ser pagadas (por cheque o en
efectivo y por quién), aprobar un presupuesto o autorizar
la comisión ejecutiva que lo haga.

g. Reportero(a)
Informa a los miembros de exhibiciones, conferencias,
conciertos, dramas, películas, etc., que sean de interés
para el Club de español. También informará sobre las
actividades del club al resto de la escuela o a la comunidad
através de periódicos, carteles, radio, etc.

Sección 3. Elección de los oficiales
Se eligen los oficiales dos veces al año, al comenzar cada
término escolar.

Artículo V. Comités
Sección 1. Los comités son:
a. Comité de programa
b. Comité especial
c. Comité de planificación
d. Comité de reglamentos

Sección 2. Las responsabilidades de los comités son:

a. Comité de programa
Este comité organiza y planea las actividades del club;
envuelve a todos los miembros en las actividades; ayuda
al club a proveer los servicios y actividades que éste
promete; envuelve a los miembros en la planificación,
organización, trabajo, responsabilidades y en la
organización de programas para las reuniones regulares;
presenta a los visitantes; consigue el equipo audiovisual,
conferenciantes, juegos, bailes, etc. El tercer
vicepresidente preside este comité.

f. Treasurer
The treasurer collects dues, distributes membership cards
to paid-up members, and keeps records of all business
transactions and up-to-date records on club expenses
incurred by individuals and committees. The treasurer files
a monthly statement and a yearly report, or upon request of
the executive committee, any time during the year. The
club should authorize the method by which bills are paid
(whether by check or by cash and by whom), approve the
budget, or authorize the executive committee to do so.

g. Reporter
The reporter calls members' attention to current exhibits,
lectures, concerts, plays, movies, etc., of interest to the
Spanish Club. He or she will report on the activities of the
club to the entire school or community through
newspapers, flyers, radio, etc.

Section 3. Election of Officers
Twice a year the members elect the officers, at the
beginning of each school term.

Article V. Committees
Section 1. The committees are:
a. Program Committee
b. Special Committee
c. Planning Committee
d. Bylaws Committee

Section 2. The duties of the committees are:

a. Program Committee
This committee plans and oversees the club's activities;
involves all members in the activities of the club; helps the
club provide the services and activities that it promises;
involves the club members in planning, organizing, taking
on responsibility, and executing tasks; plans programs for
all regular meetings; introduces visitors; arranges for
audiovisual equipment, speakers, games, dances, etc. The
third vice president serves as chairperson of this
committee.

b. Comité especial
Nombrado por el presidente bajo términos provisionales,
este comité se encarga de intereses especiales dentro del
grupo. Se encarga de la decoración, la publicidad para
acontecimientos especiales, refrescos, etc.

c. Comité de planificación
Este comité se encarga de formular una lista de posibles
actividades.

d. Comité de reglamentos
Este comité es responsable de escribir los reglamentos.
Tiene que recordar las tres cosas que las reglas de una
organización están diseñadas a hacer: delinear la
estructura de la organización, otorgar el control político y
de programa a la membresia y describir las
responsabilidades delegadas a los miembros de la
Comisión ejecutiva. Una vez que el comité termine su
trabajo, el paso final es la aceptación por los miembros del
club. El segundo vicepresidente preside el comité de
reglamentos.

Sección 3. La persona que preside un comité es responsable del
éxito del mismo.

Artículo VI. Reuniones
Sección 1. El Club de español se reunirá cada dos semanas.

Sección 2. Los oficiales y el (la) consejero(a) determinarán el
día, hora y lugar de cada reunión y se lo anunciarán a los
miembros con anticipación.

Artículo VII. Cuota
Sección 1. La cuota anual para los miembros del club será
$_____.

Sección 2. Al pagar la cuota cada miembro recibirá la tarjeta y
el manual del club.

Artículo VIII. Los colores del club
Sección 1. Los colores del Club de español son: _____,
_____ y _____.

b. Special Committees
Appointed by the president on a temporary basis, special committees take care of special interests arising in the group. These committees may be in charge of decorations, publicity for special events, refreshments, etc.

c. Planning Committee
The planning committee is responsible for compiling a list of possible activities.

d. Bylaws Committee
This committee is responsible for writing the bylaws. It must keep in mind the three things which the governing rules of a membership organization are designed to do: outline the structure of the organization, place the final control of policy and program in the membership as a whole, and specify the responsibilities delegated to members of the Executive Council. Once the committee has finished its work, the final step is acceptance by the members. The second vice president is the chairperson of the Bylaws Committee.

Section 3. The chairperson of a committee is responsible for the success of the committee.

Article VI. Meetings
Section 1. The Spanish Club will meet every two weeks.

Section 2. The officers and the adviser will determine the day, time, and place of each meeting, and let the members know in advance.

Article VII. Dues
Section 1. Membership dues for the club will be
$_____ every year.

Section 2. Each member will receive a membership card and the club handbook upon payment of dues.

Article VIII. Club Colors
Section 1. The colors for the Spanish Club are _____,
_____, and _____.

Artículo IX. La flor del club
   Sección 1. La flor del Club de español es _____.

Artículo X. Lema
   Sección 1. El lema del Club de español es _____.

Artículo XI. La canción del Club de español
   Sección 1. La canción del Club de español es _____.

Artículo XII. Enmiendas
   *Sección 1. Enmiendas a estos reglamentos requieren dos terceras partes de los
      votos. Una copia de las enmiendas a considerarse se tiene que proveer a
      cada miembro con suficiente anticipación antes de votar.*

2. Agenda (Modelo)

- *El presidente declara la sesión abierta*
- *La canción del club*
- *El lema del club*
- *Acta de la reunión anterior (Las minutas)*
- *Reportes*
   Tesorero(a)
   Comités (presentados por la persona que preside el comité)
   Secretario(a) (correspondencia)
- *Asuntos pendientes (continuación de la reunión anterior)*
- *Asuntos nuevos*
- *Se levanta la sesión*
- *Programa del día*
- *Anuncios (fecha, hora y lugar de la próxima reunión)*
- *Actividad social*
- *Refrigerios*

3. Acta o las minutas (Modelo)

Article IX. Club Flower
    Section 1. The Spanish Club flower is _____.

Article X. Motto
    Section 1. The Spanish Club motto is _____.

Article XI. Club Song
    Section 1. The Spanish Club song is _____.

Article XII. Amendment
    Section I. Amendment to these bylaws requires a two-thirds majority of votes. A copy of the proposed amendment must be provided to each member sufficiently in advance of voting.

2. Sample Agenda

- Call to order
- Club song
- Club motto
- Minutes of the preceding meeting
- Reports
  Treasurer
  Report of the committees (committee chairperson)
  Secretary (correspondence)
- Old business (continued from last meeting)
- New business
- Adjournment of business meeting
- Program of the day
- Announcements (date, time, and location of next meeting)
- Social activity
- Refreshments

3. Sample Minutes

The minutes of the Spanish Club need to be written in English, for the benefit of people outside of the club and for those who are just learning Spanish. A Spanish version of these sample minutes is included.

Acta (Minutas) del Club de Español

La segunda reunión del Club de español Cervantes *se llevó a cabo el día 5 de octubre de 19_____, en la cafetería de la escuela. La reunión comenzó a las 6:30 de la tarde.*
    Estuvieron presentes:

_____   _____

_____   _____

_____   _____

_____   _____

representando éstos un quórum de los miembros.
    El presidente declaró la reunión abierta, le siguió la canción del club y el lema. La secretaria comenzó la reunión con la lectura del acta (las minutas) de la reunión anterior. El acta (las minutas) fue aprobada por todos los presentes.

La agenda de la reunión

La reunión fue una sesión de trabajo, con la siguiente agenda:
1. *Lectura del reporte del tesorero. El tesorero reportó que el balance en la tesorería era de $55.60 y que el club necesitaba más de $95.00 para la actividad del mes entrante.*
2. *El reporte del comité de programa fue presentado por el presidente del comité; éste fue seguido por el reporte del comité especial.*
3. *Los asuntos pendientes fueron finalizados y se decidió que la fiesta de la víspera de Todos los Santos ("Halloween") se iba a celebrar en la cafetería de la escuela.*
4. *Para los asuntos nuevos fue sugerido comenzar a trabajar en la decoración para la fiesta. La sugerencia fue adoptada y se declaró el resto de la reunión como sesión de trabajo.*
5. *Los siguientes anuncios se presentaron: La próxima reunión tendrá lugar en el salón 27, el próximo martes a las 6:30 de la noche. Se presentará a un invitado que va a hablar sobre el idioma español en los Estados Unidos; también se presentará una película.*
    Al no tener más asuntos que discutir, la reunión fue, bajo moción apropiada, cerrada a las 7:30 de la noche. Se sirvieron refrigerios.

Minutes of the Spanish Club

The second meeting of the Spanish Club "Cervantes" was held on
October 5, 19_____, in the school cafeteria. The meeting started at
6:30 P.M.
    In attendance were:

_____   _____

_____   _____

_____   _____

_____   _____

being a quorum of the members.
    The president called the meeting to order, followed by the club's
song and the motto. The meeting started with the reading of the minutes
from the previous meeting by the secretary. These were approved by
all present.

Meeting Agenda

This meeting was a working meeting, with the following agenda:
1. Reading of the treasurer's report.
    The treasurer reported that the balance in the treasury was $55.60 and
that the club needed more than $95.00 for next month's activity.
2. The report of the Program Committee was read by the chairperson,
followed by the report of the special committee.
3. The old business was finalized with the agreement that the
Halloween party will be held in the school cafeteria.
4. For the new businesses it was suggested that work be started on the
decorations for the party. The suggestion was adopted, declaring the
rest of the meeting a workshop.
5. The following announcements were made: the next meeting will be
held in room 27, next Tuesday at 6:30 P.M. A speaker from Spain will
talk about the Spanish language in the United States, and there will
be a film.
    There being no further business before the meeting, the
same was on motion, duly adjourned at 7:30 P.M. Refreshments
were served.

Spanish Resources and Activities

4. Reporte del tesorero (Modelo)

Reporte del tesorero

La cantidad en la tesorería es:

Ingresos
  Balance anterior $ 20.00
  Feria de verano   40.00
  Festival español   25.00

  Total $ 85.00

Gastos
  Iniciación (8-15) $ 18.00
  Refrigerios   15.00
  Tarjetas nuevas de membresía   5.00
  Materiales para cartelones   7.50

  Total $ 45.50

Balance nuevo $ 39.50

Fecha   Tesorero(a)

Presidente(a)

4. Sample Treasurer's Report

The treasurer needs to keep an accurate financial record of the club. This report is to be presented to the members of the club every month or every time the Executive Council requires it.

Treasurer's Report

The amount in the treasury is as follows:

Earnings

Previous balance	$ 20.00
Summer fair	40.00
Spanish festival	25.00
Total	$ 85.00

Expenditures

Initiation (8-15)	$ 18.00
Refreshments	15.00
New membership cards	5.00
Material for posters	7.50
Total	$ 45.50

New Balance	$ 39.50

_____   _____
    Date   Treasurer

                           _____
                           President

5. Informe de tesorería

Fecha: _____	*Cantidad incluída* $_____._____
$_____._____ *recibido*	*Fuente:* _____
$_____._____ *gastado*	*Razón:* _____
Firma: _____	*Posición:* _____

Favor de incluir recibos envueltos en la transacción.

6. Dirigiendo la reunión

La reunión se declara abierta por el presidente.

El presidente:
1. *Secretario, por favor, ¿puede usted leer las minutas de la reunión anterior?*
2. *¿Alguna enmienda?*

El reporte mensual del tesorero es llamado seguido por los reportes de los comités.

El presidente:
3. *El tesorero va a presentar su reporte mensual.*
4. *El comité permanente va a presentar su reporte.*
5. *Ya escucharon el reporte. ¿Hay alguna sugerencia o puntos de vista que los miembros quieren presentar?*

5. Treasurer's Form

To make the treasurer's task easier and more accurate, it is necessary to have a form to report the earnings or expenditures of each committee. Each committee chairperson is responsible for filling out this financial form. It should be short and easy to fill out.

Date:_____	Total Enclosed $_____._____
$_____._____ Received	Source:_____
$_____._____ Spent	Reason:_____
Signature:_____	Position:_____

Please attach the receipts involved in the transactions.

6. Conducting the Meeting

The meeting is called to order by the president.

The president:
1. Would the secretary please read the minutes of the last meeting?
2. Are there any additions or corrections?

The monthly treasurer's report is called, followed by reports of the committees.

The president:
3. The treasurer will now give the monthly report.
4. The standing committee will present its report.
5. You have heard the report. Are there other suggestions or points of view from the members?

Lo próximo son los asuntos pendientes.

El presidente:
  6. *Los reportes de los comités se han presentado. ¿Quedan asuntos pendientes?*

El presidente:
  7. *Vamos a empezar los asuntos nuevos. ¿Hay algún anuncio? ¿Algún asunto nuevo a ser presentado?* **El programa es parte de la reunión. El presidente de cada comité da un reporte.**

El presidente:
  8. *La parte de negocios de la reunión se ha terminado; ahora procederemos al programa.*
  9. *En vista de que no hay más asuntos nuevos, se presenta la moción para cerrar la reunión.*
 10. *La reunión queda cerrada.*

7. Elección de los oficiales

Unfinished business is next in order.

The president:
  6. The reports of the committee have been presented. Is there unfinished business?

The unfinished business is presented and completed.

The president:
  7. Let's go on to the new business. Are there any announcements? Any new business to be presented? **The program is part of the meeting. The president presides, but the program chairperson makes the report.**

The president:
  8. The business part of the meeting is over, now we proceed to the program.
  9. In view of no new business, a motion for adjournment is in order.
  10. The meeting is adjourned.

7. Electing Officers

Before the meeting to elect officers, an Election Committee is appointed by the president to be in charge of the election. General rules for the election are established and announced by this committee at the time of election. The following are sample guidelines:
  1. The nominees must be notified in advance of the election meeting that they have been nominated; their consent is needed.
  2. A nominee may withdraw his or her name at any time, but cannot withdraw in favor of another member.
  3. The motion to close nominations is not in order until the meeting has been given reasonable time to add more nominations.
  4. A member may write in the name of a person that he or she wishes to vote for, whether nominated or not.
  5. The election process is by ballot.
  6. The outgoing officers continue to serve until the end of the meeting, or through the time established by the bylaws.

Reunión para elecciones (Modelo)

Presidente: *Hoy vamos a elegir a los oficiales para el año entrante. La persona que preside el comité de elecciones tiene la palabra.*

Persona a cargo del comité: *La reunión está abierta para nominaciones. Cada miembro del club tiene una lista de candidatos. ¿Hay alguna otra nominación? Una moción ha sido presentada y aceptada para cerrar nominaciones.*

Persona a cargo del comité: *Las nominaciones están cerradas; procederemos a votar. El presidente tiene la palabra.*

Presidente: *(Después de contar las papeletas) Estoy muy contento en informarles que el Sr. (la Srta.) _____, ha sido elegido(a) presidente(a) por la mayoría de los votos. Le entrego mi oficina a usted a partir de _____ (fecha).*

El mismo proceso continuará hasta que todos los oficiales sean elegidos. Después se presentará una moción para el cierre de la reunión.

8. Presentando y pasando una moción

Moción

Miembro: *Propongo que el lugar para las reuniones del Club de español sea cambiado a otro salón porque el número de miembros está aumentando.*

Otro miembro: *Secundo la moción.*

Discusión

Presidente: *Una moción ha sido presentada y secundada. La moción está abierta a discusión. ¿Quiere alguien la palabra?*

Miembro: *Yo pido la palabra. Propongo cerrar la discusión.*

Presidente: *El Sr. _____ tiene la palabra. ¿Quiere alguien la palabra? La discusión queda cerrada. Procederemos a votar.*

Sample Election Meeting

President: Now we must elect the officers for the coming year. The chairperson of the Election Committee has the floor.

Chairperson: The floor is open for nominations. Club members have a list of nominees. Are there any other nominations from the floor? A motion has been made and seconded to close nominations.

Chairperson: Nominations are closed; we will proceed to vote. The president has the floor.

President: (After ballot count.) It's my pleasure to announce that Mr. (Miss) _____, by majority of the votes, has been elected president. I turn my office over to him/her effective _____.

This process will continue until all the officers are elected. Then a motion for adjournment is presented.

8. Making and Passing a Motion

Motion

Member: I move that the place for the Spanish Club meetings be changed to another room, because the number of members is increasing.

Another member: I second the motion.

Discussion

President: A motion has been made and seconded. The motion is open to discussion. Would anyone like the floor?

Member: I request the floor. I move to close the discussion.

President: Mr. _____ has the floor. Does anyone else request the floor? The debate is closed. We will proceed to vote.

Voto

Presidente: *Votaremos por papeletas. Tenemos veintiuno en favor de la moción. Dado que esto representa la mayoría (minoría), la moción es* _____.

> *adoptada por mayoría*
> *rechazada*
> *unánimemente aceptada*

9. Tarjeta del miembro

Miembro del Club de Español

Certifico que _____
es un miembro _____*(activo, honorario) en buena posición*
del Club de español.

Para el año _____   *Presidente(a)* _____

                                 Secretario(a) _____

---

10. Iniciación

Presidente: *Miembros del Club de español, les presento los futuros miembros: (Se leen los nombres.) Sr.(Srta.) Secretario(a), por favor, ¿puede leer los reglamentos del club? (en español). Muchas gracias, Sr. (Srta.)* _____*. ¿Seguirán ustedes los reglamentos del Club de español?*

Vote

President: We will vote by ballot. We have twenty-one votes in favor of the motion. Because this represents a majority (minority), the motion is
_____.

    adopted by the majority

    defeated

    unanimously adopted

9. Membership Card

Each member needs some identification with the club, especially for specific situations such as the use of the library, discounts, club activities, etc. The following is an example of a membership card, given to new members after the payment of dues and the initiation into the club. An official seal, like the school's seal or the club's logo, along with the motto, could be included.

Member of the Spanish Club

This is to certify that _____
is an _____ (active, honorary) member in good standing of the Spanish Club.

For the year _____   President_____

                              Secretary_____

---

10. Initiation

The Initiation Committee develops an official procedure for the ceremony. An example follows:

President: Members of the Spanish Club, I present the prospective members of the club to you: (Names of the new members are read.) Will the secretary please read the Bylaws of the Spanish Club (in Spanish). Thank you, Ms. _____. Do you intend to follow the bylaws of the Spanish Club?

Futuros miembros: *Sí, Sr. Presidente, los seguiremos.*

Presidente: *¿Prometen ustedes obedecer los reglamentos, cumplir con sus responsabilidades y seguir nuestros objetivos?*

Futuros miembros: *Sí, Sr. Presidente, lo prometemos.*

Presidente: *¿Entienden ustedes que cualquier desviación a su juramento los obligará a renunciar del Club de español?*

Futuros miembros: *Sí, Sr. Presidente, entendemos.*

Presidente: *Repitan el lema del club conmigo.*

Presidente y futuros miembros: *Nosotros, los nuevos miembros del Club de español prometemos:*
> *Obedecer los reglamentos.*
> *Seguir los objetivos del club.*
> *Cumplir con nuestras responsabilidades.*

Presidente: *Por parte del Club de español les damos la bienvenida y los declaramos miembros oficiales de nuestra organización. Reciban el broche y el manual del club como símbolos de juramento.*
Al finalizar la ceremonia, se pueden servir refrigerios.

Hoja de datos biográficos y de interés del miembro

Prospective members: Yes, Mr. (Madam) President, we do.

President: Do you promise: to obey the bylaws, to keep up with your responsibilities, and to follow our goals?

Prospective members: Yes, Mr. (Madam) President we do.

President: Do you understand that any deviation from this pledge will force you to resign as a member of the Spanish Club?

Prospective members: Yes, Mr. (Madam) President we understand.

President: You may now repeat the motto of the club after me. (Members repeat the club's motto.) Now, please repeat the club pledge after me.

President and prospective members: We, the new members of the Spanish Club promise:
> to follow the bylaws.
> to follow the goals of the Spanish Club.
> to keep up with our responsibilities.

President: We, the Spanish Club, welcome you as official members of our organization. Receive the handbook and the club's pin as a symbol of commitment.
> Afterwards refreshments are served.

Member's Biographical Sketch and Interest Profile

A record containing member information is kept on file. This could be filled out before initiation, providing the Initiation Committee with information about the new member to share with the rest of the club. A sample form follows.

Hoja de datos biográficos y de interés del nuevo miembro del Club de Español

*Fecha:*_____

*Apellido:*_____

*Nombre:*_____

*Fecha de nacimiento:*_____

*Lugar de nacimiento:*_____

*Dirección:*_____

*Teléfono:*_____

*Año que cursas:*_____

*Conocimientos de otro(s) idioma(s):*_____

*Pasatiempos e intereses:*_____

*Habilidades especiales:*_____

Preguntas

Describe brevemente cómo eres.

¿Estás trabajando? ¿Dónde? ¿Cuál es tu horario de trabajo?

¿Por qué te gusta el español?

¿Qué tipo de deportes haces?

¿Cuáles son tus pasatiempos?

¿Cuáles son tus metas por los próximos cuatro años?

¿Cuáles son tus planes para el verano?

¿Cómo te sentirías si tuvieras la oportunidad de ser un líder del Club de español?

¿Te gustaría ser nominado para una posición oficial del club?

Dános información adicional que te gustaría que supiéramos.

New Spanish Club Member
Biographical Sketch and Interest Profile

Date:_____

Last Name:_____

First Name:_____

Birthdate:_____

Place of birth:_____

Address:_____

Telephone:_____

Year in School:_____

Knowledge of Foreign Language(s):_____

Hobbies and Interests:_____

Special Skills:_____

Questions

Give a brief description of yourself.

Are you working? Where? Work schedule?

Why do you like the Spanish language?

What kind of sports do you practice?

What are your hobbies?

What are your goals for the next four years?

What are your plans for this summer?

How do you feel about becoming a leader in the Spanish Club?

Would you like to be nominated for an official position?

Give us any other information that you would like us to have on
   file.

11-a. Términos parlamentarios en español

Agenda—*lista ordenada de asuntos para la reunión.*

Enmienda—*modificación, cambio.*

Papeleta—*un pedazo de papel para votación.*

Reglamentos—*una serie de reglas por las cuales se rige una organización. Usado muchas veces como sinónimo de constitución.*

Declarar abierta la sesión—*el presidente declara el comienzo de la reunión.*

Presidente del comité—*preside a un comité.* .

Fondos—*el dinero en la tesorería.*

Yo propongo—*término que se usa para presentar una moción.*

Miembros—*la espina dorsal, o parte más importante, de la organización.*

Minutas/Acta—*notas oficiales del procedimiento de una reunión.*

Moción—*una propuesta de acción.*

Proponer la clausura—*una moción hecha para finalizar la reunión.*

Asuntos nuevos—*parte de agenda.*

Candidatos—*los nominados para una posición oficial.*

Oficiales—*que tienen un cargo en una organización.*

Asuntos viejos—*asuntos de la reunión anterior que no se han terminado.*

Procedimiento parlamentario—*reglas y precedentes que rigen el procedimiento de una organización.*

Presidente(a)—*preside una organización.*

Programa—*actividad que se presenta después de finalizar los asuntos de la reunión.*

Quórum—*la mayoría de los miembros u oficiales de una organización.*

Reportero—*responsable de la publicidad de una organización.*

Segundo vicepresidente—*tomará la oficina vacante del vicepresidente.*

Secretario(a)—*responsable de la administración de una organización.*

La reunión está cerrada—*cuando el presidente finaliza la reunión oficialmente.*

Las minutas están aprobadas—*todos los miembros están de acuerdo con las notas de la reunión anterior.*

La moción se perdió—*la moción no se aprobó.*

Tercer vicepresidente—*tomará la oficina vacante de segundo vicepresidente.*

11-b. Parliamentary Terms in English

Agenda—orderly outline of business items for the meeting.

Amendment—modification, change.

Ballot—slip of paper used for voting purposes.

Bylaws—a series of rules by which an organization is governed. It is at times used as a synonym for constitution.

Call to Order—the president declares the meeting open.

Committee Chairperson—presides over a committee.

Funds—the money in the treasury.

I Move—term used in proposing a motion.

Members—the backbone of an organization.

Minutes—the official record of the proceedings of a meeting.

Motion—a proposal for action.

Move to Adjourn—a motion made to close the meeting.

New Business—part of the agenda.

Nominees—candidates for an official position.

Officers—officials of an organization.

Old business—unfinished business from the preceding meeting.

Parliamentary Procedure—the rules and precedents governing the proceedings of an organization.

President—presides over an organization.

Program—activity that will be presented after the business meeting.

Quorum—a majority number of members or officers of an organization.

Reporter—responsible for the publicity of an organization.

Second Vice President—will take the first vice president's vacant office.

Secretary—responsible for the management of an organization.

The Meeting Is Adjourned—when the meeting is officially closed by the president.

The Minutes Stand Approved—everyone agrees with the records of the preceding meeting.

The Motion Is Defeated—the motion was not approved.

Third Vice President—will take the second vice president's vacant office.

Enmendar una moción—*añadir, omitir o cambiar palabras en una moción que ya existe. Se necesitan dos terceras partes de los votos para que se adopte.*

Proceder a nombrar candidatos—*nominaciones de candidatos para posiciones oficiales.*

Encomendar—*cuando una moción está considerada para ser cambiada o cuando más información se necesita; la misma es referida a un comité para consideración y reporte.*

Tener la palabra—*cuando se le da permiso a un miembro para dirigirse a la reunión.*

Tesorero(a)—*responsable de los reportes financieros.*

Tesorería—*la oficina administrada por el tesorero.*

Vicepresidente—*preside las reuniones cuando el presidente está ausente.*

To Amend a Motion—to add, omit, or change words in the original motion. Any amendment needs two-thirds of the votes to pass.

To Call for Nominations—naming candidates for official positions.

To Commit—when a motion becomes involved through amendments or when more information is needed, it will be referred to a committee for consideration and report.

To Have the Floor—when permission is granted to address the meeting.

Treasurer—person responsible for the financial reports.

Treasury—the office that the treasurer manages.

Vice President—presides at meetings when the president is absent.

3

Club Projects

1. Yearbook

The end of the school year is a perfect time to have a personal record of all Spanish Club activities. This yearbook can be called *Anuario del club* ("Club Yearbook") or *Recuerdos* ("Mementos"). This book can include pictures of the club's most successful activities, photos of the members, short stories in Spanish, and handbook material.

2. Club Magazine

This magazine may be done semiannually or annually. It might include such literary works as poems, essays, dialogues, short stories, and compositions prepared by members during the year. One section might be dedicated to interviews with distinguished Spanish-speaking persons or with members whose outstanding work record in the club merits special attention. A good interview could be done with a former club member who has continued to study Spanish after graduation. Such an interview might focus on career opportunities for the bilingual. There could be an entertainment section that would present Hispanic recipes, describe places to visit, and provide helpful vocabulary for different social occasions. Appropriate names for this magazine are: *Nosotros, La Voz, El Círculo Español,* or *La Tertulia.*

3. Newspaper

The Spanish-language newspaper can be a monthly edition. This is the responsibility of *el Comité editorial* (Editorial Committee), named at the beginning of the school year. The newspaper can serve as a learning experience to the members and motivate nonmembers to join. Different games can be presented to increase vocabulary, and members may contribute humorous stories, cartoons, and anecdotes, as well as brief articles discussing club or community problems, sports, upcoming activities, and other relevant school or community news. Appropriate names for this newspaper are *El Reportero, Amanecer, La Opinión, Don Quijote, La Velada,* or a name that honors the school or a person.

4. Library

One of the major benefits to the school or community provided by the Spanish Club is a well-developed and organized bilingual library that could offer a variety of English and Spanish books covering topics such as the geography, culture, history, customs, and language of the Spanish-speaking countries. Also a good selection of reference books like dictionaries, periodicals, magazines, and audiovisual materials (tapes, records, films, and slides) might be initiated. A list of materials could be organized under the supervision of the school librarian. Because organizing and completing a library is not easy, a committee or two should be named for this assignment. Other committee responsibilities would be to report on current relevant news articles, periodical subscriptions, Spanish pen pals, book discounts to the club or school, and a record of Spanish-English supplementary reading done by members to assist other students who need specific information. This report would be in both languages; the following is a model in Spanish.

Reporte de lectura

Autor:_____ Editora:_____

Título:_____ Año publicado:_____

Lugar:_____

Tipo de lectura:_____

¿En qué idioma lo leíste?_____

1. Resumen:_____
_____

2. Nuevo vocabulario y expresiones:_____
_____.

3. Opinión personal:_____
_____.

4. Nombre del estudiante:_____.

5. Profesor(a):_____. Fecha:_____.

---

5. Spanish Language Information Center

This Center benefits the members who are planning to continue their studies in Spanish after graduation from high school. A group of members can provide information about scholarship opportunities, foreign language requirements in college, summer programs, sample tests, career opportunities for the bilingual, studies abroad, etc.

6. Pen Pals

This project is fun to develop and gives very positive results. Four or five students may start it. The group may write to the consulates *(consulados)* of several Spanish-speaking countries and ask for addresses of schools, organizations, clubs, or groups that would be interested in corresponding with Americans of the same age who have similar interests. When the information is received, names and addresses of Spanish-speaking people interested in communicating with other students can be posted on the club's bulletin board.

7. Translation Department

Students with a superior use of both Spanish and English may wish to establish themselves as translators and interpreters. Their services might include translating letters from pen pals or other correspondence. They could serve as interpreters for new students or members of the Hispanic community with English-language problems. Finally, they might tutor other students in Spanish classes during study-hall periods or after school. Services might be announced in both the school and community newspapers or posted on a centrally located bulletin board.

8. Tertulia

This is a social gathering during which the club's members discuss specific topics about the school, community, or the club. Because discussion is carried on in Spanish only, it is an excellent opportunity to practice the language. *La tertulia* can be held in a restaurant, the school cafeteria, or a member's home. Light refreshments may be served. The group responsible for this event will make reservations, arrange what is to be served, and decide the topic of conversation and how many members are going to be present.

9. Songs

There is a rich collection of Hispanic songs, and all reflect their own country's style and folklore. The club can select music or songs according to the country or region the group wants to represent. A good source of information for this project is a Spanish-language radio station, a college music department, or a cultural center in the community. Once the songs are selected, copies of them can be distributed to the group and used in different activities.

10. Folk Dancing

This can be a very entertaining project. Three or four members could contact a dance studio that offers instruction in traditional Hispanic dances. Such classes are frequently offered in cultural centers, high school evening classes, music departments in some colleges, or by special organizations in the community. Once the group begins to develop some dancing skills, they might set up classes themselves in order to teach other interested members after school or on weekends. Traditional dances might be featured at many club gatherings.

11. Costumes

The members of the costume group should be those with sewing skills. The group may do research on costumes from various Hispanic countries. Resources are found in the library, through consulates, or travel agencies. When costumes are ready to be made, seeking help from the Home Economics Department is advisable. Traditional costumes would add an authentic touch to club activities, especially the annual fair.

12. Songs, Dances, and Costumes

This is a combination of the three previous projects. A group is put in charge of collecting songs, dances, and costumes for an end-of-school-year activity to which people outside the club could be invited. This activity can be one of the most colorful and attractive presentations of the club.

13. Crafts

Hispanics have developed a wide variety of crafts. Interested students can work together to produce craft artifacts from different countries. Research for this can be done in the library. The following are some ideas:

- *Piñatas* made of papier-mâché and brightly colored tissue or crepe paper (Mexican art)
- Ceramic pots in bright colors (Mexican art and Central American)
- Dolls representing different Spanish-speaking countries in their respective costumes
- Woodcarving (many Hispanic countries)
- Weaving (Colombia, Peru, Guatemala)
- Pots, cups, figures, made of coconuts (Puerto Rico)
- Leather goods (Argentina and Spain)

Hispanic organizations can supply information on the different arts and their techniques.

14. Fair

One of the annual activities of the Spanish Club may be a fair. This is an opportunity to present folk dances, costumes, and selected songs in Spanish. This is an outside event to which the entire school is invited. Some tables may be set up for selling crafts and food made by members and for representing various Spanish-speaking countries. (See Chapter 8.) One table may also be set up for games. The fair might coincide with a well-known Hispanic festival. (See Chapter 5.)

15. Exhibits

Exhibits may be presented on parents' night or at the end of Hispanic Week which is the week preceding September 16. The room where the club members meet is prepared as a reception area. The decor can include posters from different countries, crafts, projects done by the members of the club, and a bulletin board announcing the coming activities. As part of the reception period the following activities can be presented: films presenting different Spanish-speaking countries, refreshments, music, and a description of the program prepared for that night. Visitors receive ballots to vote for their favorite exhibit. In the library, a section can be prepared for various exhibits. Examples include collections of Hispanic stamps, coins, paintings, songs, literary works, etc. A brief description of the projects is presented by the person responsible. A short presentation about the Spanish language books available in the library will give visitors a good impression. In the cafeteria or along the halls, exhibits of Hispanic crafts and items keep the visitors interested. The auditorium is an excellent place to hold the traditional dances and the presentation of costumes. Prizes can be awarded in the auditorium ten minutes before the closing of the activity.

16. Trips to Spanish-speaking Countries

A summer trip to Spanish-speaking countries is a wonderful opportunity to expose the members to the Spanish language and Hispanic culture. These trips are expensive and need extensive preparation. With the right motivation and dedication this could be accomplished. Many fund-raising activities (see Chapter 3, Part 20) are done for this purpose, from the beginning of the year through the summer. These trips are a good opportunity to convince members that they can communicate effectively in Spanish. An introduction to the places they will visit is required preparation for the trip. Booklets with essential vocabulary and phrases are good for practice. The following are examples.

Mandatos	Orders
Quieto.	Quiet.
Esperen.	Wait.
Silencio.	Silence.
Miren.	Look.
Oigan.	Listen.
Preste atención.	Pay attention.
En la mesa.	At the table.
Buen apetito.	Enjoy your meal.
Sabe muy bien.	It tastes good.
Mesero o mesera.	Waiter or waitress.
Estoy listo para ordenar.	I am ready to order.
La cuenta, por favor.	The check, please.
Un vaso de agua, por favor.	A glass of water, please.

De compras	Shopping
Estoy mirando solamente.	I'm just looking.
¿Cuánto cuesta?	How much does it cost?
Esto es caro (barato).	It's expensive (cheap).
Me gusta esto.	I like this.
Quiero comprar...	I want to buy...
¿Es esto el precio?	Is this the price?

Direcciones	Directions
A la derecha.	To the right.
A la izquierda.	To the left.
Al doblar la esquina.	Right around the corner.
Allí.	Over there.
Al cruzar la calle.	Across the street.
En la próxima parada.	In the next stop.

Expresiones	Expressions
Tenga un buen viaje.	Have a good trip.
No se preocupe.	Don't worry.
Eso es cierto.	That's true.
¡Qué mala suerte!	What bad luck!
¡Dios lo cuide!	God bless you!
Lo sentimos mucho.	We are sorry.
¿Qué tal?	What's up?
¡Fantástico!	Fantastic!
¡Claro que sí!	Yes, indeed!
¡No tiene sentido!	Nonsense!

17. Lectures

A native Spanish speaker, a professor, or a member of the community who is knowledgeable on a topic of interest to the group may be invited to give a lecture. This may be done at least twice a year, and the public in general may be invited. This presentation may be complemented with audiovisual equipment like slides, pictures, or maps.

18. National Hispanic Week

This is an important week for the Spanish Club because it celebrates the Spanish heritage in the United States. This week is typically the one preceding September 16. Club activities should be planned for this time. A roundtable club meeting is an ideal way to begin brainstorming for this period. The group can then be divided into smaller groups, made up of three to four members each. Groups should come up with at least two activities for the week. A second round of discussion should be set up to finalize the details for each activity, including a schedule for each event, naming the Hispanic Week Committee, and making the necessary arrangements to carry out the projected activities.

19. International Day

Prior to International Day a week of activities may be planned, culminating on International Day. Through the combined efforts of various language clubs in the school or the community, the following activities can be planned: a tea party in the evening or during a free period with hostesses in native costumes to officially open the week of activities; a film festival showing classic films from different countries; a field day of competition between clubs having different traditional games and races; a bake sale in which the Spanish Club has a table representing dishes, pastries and beverages from Spanish-speaking countries; a speaker to talk about Hispanic immigrants and their language influence; an exhibition of crafts and related items; a day in which members are exchanged among the different language clubs; and a *tertulia* in which the topic of discussion could be the identification of ethnic groups in the community and their problems confronting a different culture and language. The week is closed with International Day. On this date, all the members are dressed in native costumes, and the day's activities may include contests, presentations to the rest of the school to attract members, and a luncheon with teachers and leaders of the community. To close International Day, a banquet is held during the evening. Each table can represent one country, and a member is selected as the keynote speaker. This student talks about the highlights of the week and expresses appreciation for the participation of all members. The speaker then presents awards such as certificates of achievement and appreciation. National Textbook Company provides blank certificates of merit in different languages (see appendix).

20. Fund-raising Activities

The following are possible money raising activities:
- Ads from community businesses in the club's newspaper or magazine.
- A car wash during weekends.
- A concession stand at school games or fairs.

- Bake sales during weekends or after school.
- A Halloween or Valentine's Day dance at the school cafeteria.
- A dance for the school or community.
- A book fair, selling books donated by the community.
- Chores done around the community, for example: mowing lawns, shoveling show, cleaning backyards, streets, lots, etc.
- Selling crafts or international items.
- Selling books of Hispanic recipes during the holidays.
- Making *piñatas* for parties and birthdays.
- Catering meetings or parties.
- A yard sale of items donated by the community.
- Selling box lunches during special occasions when the cafeteria is not open.
- Selling doughnuts during free periods.
- Selling candies.
- Selling Christmas cards and wrapping paper.
- Gift wrapping services during the holidays.
- Selling cakes in front of shopping centers during weekends.
- Movies in the auditorium open to the public.
- Selling popcorn or *nachos* during these movies.

21. Publicity

Publicity is the key to the success of any activity. The people for whom the activity is intended have to know about it at least one week in advance. Posters are one of the most effective ways to advertise, along with flyers, announcements on every school bulletin board (with a brief review of the activity), the community and school newspapers, the radio as a public service, or during the morning announcements using the school intercom system.

22. Individual and Group Projects

This section is directed to individual members or groups of members who are interested in doing a project for a Spanish fair or exhibits, or for prizes at the end of the school year. The interested member may present a proposal to the adviser; the proposal shows the time involved, references, research, and goals. The adviser decides whether the proposal is a challenge to the member or the group, if it has good potential, and if it constitutes a learning experience.

Projects

- A short paper on Hispanic culture.
- A book report on a classic Spanish language novel.
- An original crossword puzzle in Spanish.
- A translation from an article on Spanish-speaking people.
- A set of posters for classroom decoration.
- A *piñata* for the meeting room.
- Composition of a short song or poem in Spanish.
- A list of Spanish language proverbs.
- A scrapbook of articles on Hispanic countries.
- Hispanic recipes with English translations.
- An interview with a Spanish-speaking person from the community, conducted in Spanish.
- A presentation of a book report to the group, in Spanish.
- A cultural presentation using audiovisual material.
- A short skit about a travel agent who tries to convince a client to visit a Spanish-speaking country. The agent needs to present information about each country he or she is promoting.
- Research and presentation of some differences in food and traditional costumes among Spanish-speaking countries.
- A list of Spanish surnames and the country of origin.
- A chart with the conjugations of ten irregular verbs.
- A list of Spanish words adopted by American speech.
- A cartoon strip with Spanish captions to be published in the club's magazine.
- The presentation of an original Spanish language activity that the group could adapt.
- The creation of a song to teach the Spanish alphabet.
- A list of colleges that offer a degree in Spanish and their corresponding entrance requirements.
- A game idea involving the learning of Spanish prepositions.
- An original Spanish script for a play involving about five characters, taking place in Mexico or Spain with references to important places.
- Research and a presentation of the currency used in the different Spanish-speaking countries.

4

Programs

1. Travelogues *(Presentaciones sobre viajes)*

Members who have traveled to Spanish-speaking countries and have slides of the trip could prepare a slide presentation for the group. One person shows the slides and a second person narrates. It is a good idea to set a time limit for the presentation.

2. Game Programs *(Programas de juegos)*

Game sessions are very enjoyable. The games need to involve learning experiences and the use of Spanish. Some sample games are presented in Chapter 6.

3. Party Decorations *(Decoraciones para fiestas)*

Making decorations can be more fun than the party itself. Students bring materials such as scissors, masking tape, paint, brushes, and any other items needed to make the decorations.

4. Birthday Parties *(Fiestas de cumpleaños)*

To celebrate the birthdays of famous personalities, the program could begin with a presentation of the person's life and work. The presentation should include audiovisual materials. A map could be used to show the country and area where the person comes from, a slide presentation showing the person's work, native music, etc. The local library might have information on many Hispanic personalities. The meeting concludes with refreshments, including a birthday cake for the occasion. The decor of the room includes balloons and crepe paper.

5. Festival Programs *(Programa de festivales)*

Hispanic festivals, or *fiestas,* are full of fun and traditions. There is at least one major festival for each month of the year in some part of the Spanish-speaking world. Most *fiestas* can be traced to a religious origin. For these celebrations, costumes are used and music is an important part of the event. Some festivals are:

- Día de los Reyes (January)
- La Candelaria (February)
- Fiesta de las Cruces (March—April)
- Cinco de Mayo (May)
- Día de San Juan (June)
- Lunes del Cerro (July)
- Assumption (August)
- Mexican and Chilean Independence Day (September)
- Día de la Raza (October)
- Día de todos los Santos y Día de los Difuntos (November)
- Navidad (December)

Ideas for some of these programs are presented in Chapter 5.

6. Coffee Circle *(Tertulia)*

This is a simple meeting for an informal conversation, around coffee, tea, sodas, or juices. Topics of conversation could be the details of an activity, problems involving the club or community, or a conversation with an invited guest. The meeting could be held in the school cafeteria, the library, or a house or restaurant.

7. Sports Programs *(Programa de deportes)*

An evening can be dedicated to sports. The group is divided in two; one group may be named *Los Valientes* and the other, *Los Campeones*. Both groups play for points; the losers must buy refreshments for the winners. Games such as volleyball, tennis, racquetball, baseball, etc., are played. This could be done twice a month.

8. Orientation Programs *(Programas de orientación)*

An Orientation Program offers information to club members on a variety of subjects. At the beginning of the year a list of topics of interest is prepared by all members. During the year people knowledgeable about particular topics are contacted and invited to talk to the group. The following are possible subjects:

- *Language careers.* A counselor from a high school or college can be contacted.
- *Travel.* A representative of a travel agency could be invited to talk about planning trips to Latin American countries and Spain.
- *Hispanic music.* A disk jockey from a Spanish language radio station could come in and talk about Hispanic music.
- *Hispanic food.* A chef from a Hispanic restaurant could do a demonstration of that restaurant's cuisine before interested members.

9. Rehearsal Program *(Sesión de ensayo)*

Many of the club's activities need rehearsals. A schedule for this program needs to be set up to avoid wasting time; if possible, the rehearsal should be at the same place as the activity.

10. Campfire Program *(Fogata)*

A *fogata* is an excellent occasion to sing Spanish songs, play games, and practice the language. It could take place close to a river, or on a beach during a clear night. Mystery stories could be told (Hispanic legends can be found in the library) around the campfire. A few days before the activity, a member of the group should be named by the adviser to research those legends or superstitions, without the knowledge of the rest of the group. During the evening of the *fogata*, the person with the stories waits until everyone is around the fire, sets the mood for mystery, and then begins to tell the stories. This is a good activity for the month of October.

11. Folk Dance Demonstration
(Demostración de bailes típicos)

The club could invite a Spanish cultural group to present a demonstration of traditional dances. A large room such as the auditorium is needed for this purpose. After the demonstration a question and answer session is indicated. Afterwards, *refrescos* and *entremeses* are served.

5

Themes

This chapter describes a series of festivals that take place throughout Latin America or Spain on specific dates. Most of these festive occasions have religious origins. The club could adapt these festivities as themes for programs or special activities.

1. Epiphany (*Día de los Reyes*)

January 6 is *el Día de los Reyes*, known in English-speaking countries as Epiphany or the Twelfth Day of Christmas. It is primarily a children's holiday. On this day, they receive gifts from the Three Kings. Typically on January 5, children place hay and water in their homes as food for the Wise Men's camels. The next morning the children find gifts stuffed inside the shoes they had also laid out for the Three Kings. In Mexico, children's parties are celebrated for this holiday, with the traditional *piñata*.

As an activity for the club during this time, members could hold a drawing of names to exchange inexpensive presents. Small boxes with hay, properly identified with the owner's name, are left under a Christmas tree or *nacimiento*. Members dressed as Kings appear and replace the hay with a present in each box. After everyone receives a present, a *piñata* is broken.

2. Day of Candlemas (*Día de la Candelaria*)

Candelaria means "purification with fire." This holiday occurs in February and commemorates the purification of the Virgin Mary. The Virgin of

Candelaria is the patron saint of Bolivia, Cartagena (Colombia), and Tlacotalpan (Mexico). This is a day for a series of traditional religious observances. During the evening the children make a fire *(una fogata)* in a safe area and circle it singing songs.

As an activity for the club, a campfire program could be organized during February, weather permitting.

3. Carnivals *(Carnavales)*

Carnivals in Latin America and Spain are celebrated before Lent, usually around the end of February or during March. The best-known carnival, of course, is the one in Rio de Janeiro. But other cities also celebrate this time with music and parades; the *Mardi Gras* in New Orleans is just one example. These festivals are celebrated with extraordinary parades featuring huge floats. People wear masks that represent all kinds of grotesque characters and evil spirits; women may wear extravagant costumes; and participants perform dances, tricks, and games for the spectators.

Carnivals are also celebrated at this time in Panama (Panama City), Colombia (Barranquilla), Venezuela (Caracas), Peru, Ecuador, Bolivia, Mexico, and Puerto Rico. To celebrate *Carnavales* the Spanish Club can plan a costume ball. A parade to open the activity is prepared, with the queen and king of the carnival preceding the group. Floats can be made using huge drawings on cardboard and having various members carry them. Members can prepare their own carnival masks and costumes.

Other Spanish clubs may be invited to participate and the public may attend as spectators. If the number of participants is substantial, it is a good idea to have the parade outside ending with the costume ball. The decor can consist of posters showing the carnival, evil figures, or places where the carnivals take place.

4. Tribute to Spain *(Día de España)*

Spain celebrates a variety of *festivales, verbenas,* and *romerías,* usually to honor the patron saint of the city or town. Parades, floats, typical music and dances, and food fests may all be part of the festivities.

A program presenting a dance in combination with a *fiesta española* may take place in the auditorium or a large room. Regional costumes or those representing typical characters may be used. Spanish dances and music are the heart of the *fiesta.* The decor could be a fruit and vegetable stand, *una vendedora de flores* selling fresh flowers; *un sereno* patrolling the street and calling the hour; *unas señoritas* followed by *un galán; una gitana* telling *la buenaventura;* girls dancing the songs played by *el joven guitarrista.*

5. The Fifth of May *(El cinco de mayo)*

One of Mexico's most important national holidays is the fifth of May. It commemorates the victory of the Mexican forces over the French Army at Puebla in 1862. This fiesta is celebrated in Mexico and the United States by Mexican-Americans. This celebration includes parades, dances, and food festivals. The parade consists of floats representing different parts of Mexico, costumes, bands, and dances. The popular *Mariachis* wearing the traditional costumes of *el charro* play *Las Rancheras* and *música romántica*. The club can contact Mexican-Americans from the community and organize a *fiesta*. If it is already organized by the Mexican community, a request for participation by the members of the club could be made. This is an excellent learning experience. The participants could wear Mexican costumes and only Spanish will be used.

6. Feast of St. John *(Día de San Juan)*

This feast, on June 24, is celebrated throughout the Hispanic world in a number of ways. In areas of South America where it is winter, people gather around bonfires for one of the biggest celebrations of winter. North of the equator—for instance, in Puerto Rico and the coastal areas of South America—people rush to the nearest beach and walk backwards into the water three times for a ritual bath and to release evil spirits. This is typically done at midnight the night of June 23 to insure good luck for the whole year. Superstitions abound during this time: one example is to crack open an egg, pouring the contents into a glass filled with water, and to let the glass set overnight; by morning on June 24, the egg is supposed to form a specific figure that is used to interpret the near future. The figure of an airplane or a ship means a trip in the near future.

The activity for this celebration could be held outdoors with a bonfire at night, or a picnic around a pool or at the beach. For an indoor program, each member could pour an egg inside a glass of water and during *El día de San Juan* a discussion about this superstition might take place using the results of the egg.

7. Independence Day in Peru *(Día de la Independencia del Perú)*

From July 28 to August 1, Peru celebrates its independence. Typical celebrations include street fairs, bullfights, parades of elaborate floats, and fireworks. A program to celebrate this occasion might consist of a presentation on Peru and its people. A bulletin board could be dedicated to the country with interesting information and pictures.

8. Assumption Day *(Día de la Asunción)*

August 15 commemorates the assumption of the *Virgen María* into heaven. Celebrations vary from Masses to very colorful parades, which take place in Mexico and Guatemala. A discussion about religious customs in Latin America and Spain and the influence they exercise on people's lives can be a good program for this day. Slides or a film presentation of these festivities can be part of the discussion.

9. Day of the Charros *(Día de los Charros)*

September 14 is reserved for Mexico's national hero, the *charro*. On this day, a parade and *jaripeo* (rodeo) is held. The *jaripeo* has at least ten different events, with *charros* participating in those of their preference. A combined program might be developed to celebrate the Day of the Charros and Mexican Independence Day since both dates are close and both take place in Mexico.

10. Mexican Independence Day *(Día de la Independencia de México)*

In Mexico, September 16 has been established as National Independence Day, and every September 15 at 11 P.M., Father Miguel Hidalgo's call to arms (known as *el Grito de Dolores)* is reenacted in every city and town of Mexico.

To celebrate this date the club can invite a speaker from Mexico to talk about *La Independencia de México* and *El Día de los Charros*. The decor of the room will include posters, ceramics from Mexico, and *piñatas*. After the formal presentation is over, a small fiesta is offered in honor of the guest and *La Independencia de México* with *música mexicana, piñatas,* and *refrescos* such as "mock" *sangría* (a fruit punch), *tostitos, chiles, jalapeños, frijoles* (refried beans), or *una torta*.

11. Chilean Independence Day *(Día de la Independencia de Chile)*

Chile celebrates its independence on September 18 with parades and dances. To use this theme in a program, a group of members can be assigned to write to the Chilean Consulate for information about the country's history, people, culture, music, and economy. The group may want to point out the differences that exist between Chile and the other Latin American countries. When enough material is obtained, a panel discussion can be presented to the rest of the members, ending with a question and answer session.

Some students may wish to make either a written or an oral report to the Club on one or all of the following Hispanic holidays.

12. Feast of St. Francis of Assisi *(Fiesta de San Francisco de Asís)*

This is celebrated on October 4, and a number of *fiestas* in his honor are held throughout Latin America and Spain.

13. Columbus Day *(Día de la Raza)*

October 12 is celebrated throughout the Spanish-speaking world to honor the ancestry, language, religion, and culture that are shared by so many. Speeches and parades highlight this day. In Santo Domingo (Dominican Republic), the casket of Cristóbal Colón is put on display.

14. All Saints' Day and All Souls' Day *(Día de todos los santos y Día de los difuntos)*

November 1 is All Saints' Day and November 2 is All Souls' Day. Both celebrations are of a highly religious nature. All Saints' Day honors all Christian saints, especially those who do not have feast days. Catholics must attend Mass on this day. November 2 is a special time for offering prayers and Mass for souls in purgatory. It is customary to visit the graves of loved ones and place flowers on them. For this holiday, many flower vendors set up temporary stands to sell their goods.

15. December

The month of December is observed with both secular and Christian celebrations. *Nacimientos, pesebres, árboles de navidad, villancicos, piñatas, aguinaldos,* and the preparation of special foods are all signs that it is mid-December and everyone is ready for Christmas. All Hispanic countries celebrate this special time of year according to their own traditions.

In Colombia, the Christmas season opens on December 16 when friends gather at each other's homes in the evening to celebrate *la novena.* They sing Spanish carols known as *villancicos,* pray at *un pesebre,* and later have dinner and dance at home. In Oaxaca, Mexico, the pre-Christmas activities begin on the twenty-third with a special celebration called *Noche de rábanos* during which people dressed in typical costumes gather around the *zócalo* or *plaza.* Around it, everything is decorated with huge radishes carved into extraordinary forms resembling animals or people. It is typical to eat *buñuelos* at this time.

In Paraguay and Peru, *los nacimientos* are usually not displayed until December 24. In many parts of Mexico, they are left up until January 6, which is when the Wise Men finally reach the Holy Family.

On *Nochebuena* all celebrations reach a climax. In Mexico and Central America the last *posada* is highlighted by special parades. In many communities in Venezuela, people dress as shepherds and shepherdesses and go from house to house singing *villancicos.* In Costa Rica, the midnight celebration is purely secular. People wear masks and march along the main street of the capital, scattering confetti. At midnight on Christmas Eve, outdoor activities come to an end. Catholics hurry to church for the *Misa de gallo* (Midnight Mass) which celebrates the birth of Jesus. After Mass, families return home for a special Christmas supper. Turkey, lamb, and roast pig are among the more traditional foods served.

Tables in Venezuela proudly display the *hallacas, jamón planchado,* and *dulce de lechoza.* In Mexico the families always look for *tamales* with either chocolate, fruit, or chicken fillings, each one corresponding to a particular *barrio,* or section, of the city. Panamanians also serve *tamales* and sweet sausages cooked in wine accompanied by fruit bread. Nicaraguans prepare the famous *sopa borracha* (drunken soup), and the *nacatamales.* In Argentina, there is the traditional *torta* made with flour, eggs, raisins, and nuts. In Chile a favorite main dish is lobster brought especially from the Juan Fernández Islands.

Christmas Day is very quiet; all of the members of the family gather together for a day of relaxation and conversation. Holiday activities continue until January 6, with the celebration of *El día de los Reyes* (Three King's Day) which is the traditional day for giving gifts. Children write letters to the *Tres Reyes Magos,* asking them for gifts. In Madrid, several days before Epiphany, there is a parade (complete with camels) to honor the Kings' arrival. Parents bring their children who later have a chance to ask the Kings to bring them presents.

The activity of the Spanish Club for the month of December could involve decorating the room with a simple *nacimiento*, featuring images of Jesus, Mary, and Joseph. For a more ambitious project, figures of the Three Wise Men, angels, shepherds, sheep, and other animals may be added. These figures can be made of various materials (clay, wood, plaster, rubber, or cardboard). The *nacimiento* may be placed under a Christmas tree or in a prominent place in the room. Different types of *piñatas* may also be hung in the classroom. A day is selected to celebrate Christmas Eve. On that day, members can wear typical costumes and sing *villancicos* around the *nacimiento*. Afterwards, refreshments are served and the *piñatas* are broken.

6

Games

This chapter is dedicated to games that can be played in the classroom or in any other place where the club meets. The games provide both learning experiences and entertainment. Each game requires use of the language, so that students' mastery of Spanish will be enhanced.

1. Simon Says (*Simón dice*)

A leader is chosen for the game, and the players stand in a semicircle facing him or her. Speaking very rapidly, the leader gives commands to the group; the players do everything the leader says when the comand is preceded by *Simón dice*. However, if the phrase *Simón dice* is left out, they must not obey. The leader makes rapid commands such as: *Simón dice brazos hacia arriba; Simón dice las manos a la cabeza; Simón dice una pierna levantada; Simón dice la cabeza levantada; Simón dice que den una vuelta alrededor del salón.* After these, the leader says *Manos a la cara.* The player who obeys the last command loses and must drop out of the game or do whatever has been established as a penalty at the beginning of the game.

2. *Letras del alfabeto*

To play this game, the group needs pieces of paper about two inches square and either safety pins or masking tape. Each letter of the Spanish alphabet, except *x*, is written on a piece of paper. Letters can be repeated to accommodate a large number of players, or two letters per person may be given if the group is small. A piece of paper with a letter is pinned or taped on the front of each player. At a given signal, the game begins: One player asks another a question in Spanish and starts counting out loud in Spanish from one to ten. The player who has been asked the question must answer with a word beginning with the letter that is written on his own piece of paper before *diez* is reached. If a correct answer is given, the questioner attaches his letter on the player; if no answer is given, the player who failed to answer must give up his letter to the questioner. If the loser has another letter previously captured, or if two letters were assigned at the beginning, he or she may now pin it on; if not, the player drops out of the game. The player with the greatest number of letters at the end of the game is the winner. This game is an excellent way to develop vocabulary in specific areas such as science and mathematics. For example, words beginning with *a* in mathematics: *ángulo, agudo, área, adición*, etc.; words with *c* in science: *corazón, capilares, células, cerebro*, etc.

3. *Presente, pasado y futuro*

You will need paper and pencil for this game. A time limit of twenty minutes to half an hour should be assigned. A leader is selected from the group. A piece of paper is given to each player, and the leader asks the players to write their names on it and then to fold the paper so that the name cannot be seen. The papers are then passed three times from one player to another, with each one writing on the paper and then folding it again. When the paper has been folded once, the player must write something concerning *el presente*, fold the paper a second time and pass it to the next player. Papers folded twice are ready for something concerning *el pasado*; and those folded three times must carry something about *el futuro*. No one is allowed to read what has already been written under the folds. When everyone is finished, the papers are collected; the leader reads the paper, beginning with the name. The following are some possible comments made by the players:

Presente

- *Está enamorado de Dulcinea.*
- *Está tomando clases de baile con una escoba de maestra.*
- *Está escribiendo un libro de español usando solamente el verbo amar.*
- *Cree que la diferencia entre hoja y ojo es que hoja es la esposa del ojo.*

Pasado

- *Dio el comparativo y el superlativo de ''enfermo'' como: enfermo, peor, muerto.*
- *Una vez le ofrecieron cola y aceptó creyendo que era una soda.*
- *Creía que Don Quijote era su vecino.*

Futuro

- *Va a escribir un libro titulado* Cómo estudiar sin trabajo.
- *Va a hacer una fiesta en su casa para invitar a Don Quijote y a Sancho Panza.*
- *Va a inventar un curso en español sobre cómo comunicarse en inglés.*
- *Hará un experimento para probar que el hombre salió de un huevo.*
- *Pedirá a la maestra de español que le apruebe el curso con matrícula de honor.*

4. *Los cuatro elementos*

The players form a circle; one player tosses an object, designated as a signal to begin the game, to another and calls out the name of one of the four elements: *aire, agua, fuego,* or *tierra.* If *aire* is called, the player to whom the object is tossed must mention the name of a bird before the tosser can count to ten in Spanish. An aquatic animal or fish must be named if *agua* is called out; an animal confined to land must be identified if *tierra* is mentioned. If *fuego* is called, the player in turn must say instead: *Constantinopla lindísima.* The penalty for a mistake may be dropping out of the game.

For less advanced classes the following list is helpful:

Tierra: *el hombre, el gato, el tigre, el elefante, la ardilla, el perro, el león, la zorra, el pavo, el oso.*
Aire: *el cóndor, la golondrina, el cuervo, la cotorra, el loro, el canario, la paloma, el buho, el águila, el halcón, el gorrión.*
Agua: *el atún, la sardina, el tiburón, la ballena, el salmón, el hipopótamo, el cocodrilo, la piraña, la foca, la estrella de mar.*

5. *La casa que Juan construyó*

This game is good for developing skills in pronunciation and in understanding spoken Spanish. The story is read by the leader, who must have a good knowledge of Spanish. If the class is made up of first-year students, it is a good idea for them to repeat each sentence after the leader. After a period of practice together, the first student begins, and the recital goes around the group, with each person adding a new phrase and repeating the previous phrases until the story is completed. For extra help, the leader should write the phrases on the board. If anyone makes a mistake, that player will drop out of the game until he or she feels ready to try again. Part of this game could be the development of an original story, which could be as much fun as the game itself. The story goes around as follows:

1st: *Esta es la casa que Juan construyó.*

2nd: *Este es el queso que se quedó en la casa que Juan construyó.*

3rd: *Esta es la rata que comió el queso que se quedó en la casa que Juan construyó.*

4th: *Este es el gato que cogió a la rata que comió el queso que se quedó en la casa que Juan construyó.*

5th: *Este es el perro que persiguió al gato que cogió a la rata que comió el queso que se quedó en la casa que Juan construyó.*

6th: *Esta es la vaca que encornó al perro que persiguió al gato que cogió a la rata que comió el queso que se quedó en la casa que Juan construyó.*

7th: *Esta es la muchacha que ordeñó a la vaca que encornó al perro que persiguió al gato que cogió a la rata que comió el queso que se quedó en la casa que Juan construyó.*

8th: *Este el el hombre que besó a la muchacha que ordeñó a la vaca que encornó al perro que persiguió al gato que cogió a la rata que comió el queso que se quedó en la casa que Juan construyó.*

9th: *Este es el cura que terminó este cuento casando a la muchacha con el hombre que besó a la muchacha que ordeñó a la vaca que encornó al perro que persiguió al gato que cogió a la rata que comió el queso que se quedó en la casa que Juan construyó.*

6. *¿Qué estoy viendo?*

In this game only the leader knows the secret. Before the game the leader selects a definite object in the room and asks: *¿Qué estoy viendo?* Each of the players who are seated in a circle is allowed one question and one guess. The questions could be as follows: *¿Es animal? ¿Es vegetal? ¿Es mineral? ¿Es grande? ¿Es pequeño? ¿Es masculino? ¿Es femenino? ¿Está a la derecha? ¿Está en frente de nosotros?* The only restriction is that the questions have to be answered with *Sí* or *No*. Every player will keep in mind the previous questions (and answers), as well as the guesses, to eliminate or add possibilities. The person who guesses the secret will be the next leader.

7. *Haciendo un telegrama*

The group will need prepared telegraph blanks and pencils. Each telegraph blank is prepared with ten letters, all about three quarters of an inch apart. The object of the game is to write a telegram in ten minutes, using the given letter at the beginning of the missing word. The letter *y* may be added by the player, and any letter may be capitalized. Each telegram must contain a complete sentence that is grammatically correct, though the content may be humorous or even ridiculous. At the end of ten minutes, the game is over and the "telegrams" are collected. The leader reads the telegrams aloud, and declares the cleverest one the winner. To add more enthusiasm to the game, each telegram is given back to a different player. This time, each player will try to write a telegram using different words but having the same meaning as the original.

The blanks may be prepared by assigning letters in any order. The following is an example:

f	*d*	*p*	*p*	*p*	*n*
f	*s*	*n*	*s*	*s*	*l*

This telegram might read: *Fama y dinero producen placer pero no felicidad si no se saben llevar.*

8. *Haciendo una oración*

Paper, pencils, and a few index cards with common Spanish words written on them are needed for this game. The leader will hold up the cards and show them to the players one at a time. The players use the word shown on the card to write a complete sentence on a piece of paper. The first one who finishes a correct sentence wins the card. It would be a good idea to record the time it takes to complete each sentence. All papers should be collected and checked.

If the game is played with advanced students, more difficult sentences may be required. The leader may ask that a noun be used as a subject, a direct object, or an indirect object. Irregular verbs such as *tener, hacer, haber, dar, decir, estar, ser, querer,* or *ir* could be written on the cards, each to be used in a certain tense. Verbs in the subjunctive mood are especially suitable for such a game. Question or exclamation marks could be added to the word to indicate how the player should use it in a sentence. For advanced classes, five words are used on each card, and the player is requested to develop a short paragraph using the words on the card. For example, *escuela, tarea, estudiar, televisión, reunión* could be used with these sample results:

Enseguida que termino mi tarea de la escuela, me siento a cenar con mi familia. Hablamos y luego de terminar nos sentamos a ver la televisión. Media hora antes de las 7:00 reviso la agenda para la reunión del Club de español. Al finalizar la reunión regreso a mi casa y comienzo a estudiar.

9. *Buscando palabras*

This game requires two teams of six players each, seated on opposite sides of the room. The leader counts to five, which is the signal to begin. One player from each team runs to the blackboard and writes a Spanish word from any part of speech, including proper nouns. The player then runs back to his or her seat, giving the chalk to the next player on the team, who will do the same, but with a different word. This continues until one team finishes. Duplicate words are not allowed within a team and teams may not share words.

If either team makes a mistake, it loses the game. Team places and words are switched. Now the object of the game is to identify the parts of speech to which these words belong. This should be done in the same way the words were written on the board; abbreviations should be used. The first team to finish wins.

10. *Oraciones desconocidas*

Two teams are needed for this game, with each one facing the other. The leader counts to five, and the first player on each team runs to the board, writes a Spanish word, and then sits down. Each player follows suit until all the players have written enough words on the board to make a sentence. The leader needs to set a time limit for this part of the game. Two minutes are then given to the teams to rearrange the words and write a sentence on a piece of paper. The first team to finish a complete Spanish sentence that is both coherent and grammatically correct is the winner.

11. *¿Cómo está el día hoy?*

This is a simple game that does not require a strong background in Spanish and one in which the players develop vocabulary about the weather (*calor, frío, viento, lluvia,* etc.) and the points of the compass (*norte, sur, este, oeste*).

The leader stands in front of the class and says *sur*. The class must then point in that direction. When the leader says: *este, norte,* or *oeste,* the students should point in the direction indicated. When the leader says *Hace frío,* the players act as though they are freezing. When the leader says *Hace calor,* they act accordingly. If the next word is *lluvia,* they may put their hands over their heads to ward off the rain. If the leader says *tempestad,* the players hold on to their hats and their clothes. If the word is *bueno,* they remain perfectly still.

This game is a lot of fun because it calls for originality in the students' imitations. Different types of vocabulary can be employed. For example, the names of animals could produce amusing imitations.

12. *El arco iris*

To play this game, the players need paper and pencil. A leader and seven players are selected; the seven represent the seven colors of the rainbow. The players stand in front of the class, and the leader assigns a color to each of them in the following order: *rojo, anaranjado, amarillo, verde, azul, rosado, violeta*. The other club members, who are seated, repeat the name of each color several times in unison with the leader, in order to associate the color with the person who represents it. Now everyone closes their eyes, and the leader rearranges the seven players with the assigned colors in different positions. When the other club members open their eyes, they must try to write the colors in a new order. The results are checked by having each of the seven players repeat the name of the color he or she represents. The winner or winners of the game are those who have written the new list of colors correctly.

This game could be adapted as an exercise to memorize the names of famous Hispanics. For example, the leader could read the names of seven famous writers, such as: Camilo José Cela, Gabriel García Márquez, Gabriela Mistral, Mario Vargas Llosa, Carlos Fuente, Pablo Neruda, and Julio Cortázar.

13. *Palabras mixtas*

A group of six players and a leader are selected. The leader is sent out of the room. The six players inside make up a sentence containing six words, one assigned to each player. They rearrange themselves forming a line to change the correct order of the words in the sentence. The leader is called back, and the line-up repeats the words successively, while the leader tries to unscramble the sentence. If the leader cannot rearrange the sentence the first time, he or she is allowed to ask for two more repetitions by saying *Otra oportunidad*. If the leader is still unable to unscramble the sentence, the player at the head of the line becomes the new leader and goes outside. A new sentence is made up by the remaining players, and the game is repeated. To assure a good participation of other members, the seven players should be changed every three or four sentences.

14. *Pronombres demostrativos*

The object of this game is to familiarize the students with Spanish demonstrative pronouns. The leader of the group is sent out of the room. While he or she is away, the group selects an object which must be identified by the leader. When the leader returns, he or she addresses a series of questions to each player. For example, *¿Es éste (ésta)?* if the leader touches it; *¿Es ése (ésa)?* if the object is near one of the other players; *¿Es aquél (aquélla)?* if the object is at a distance. If plural nouns are to be identified, the corresponding forms are used. The player who answers the question must be careful in doing so. For instance, if the leader says: *¿Es éste?*, the player must say: *No, no es ése.* The object chosen should be rather difficult to locate. Everyone must use correct Spanish.

15. *Usted o Tú*

This game will familiarize the players with the use of and the difference between *usted* and *tú* during a conversation in Spanish. Each player is given the name of a person, object, or animal. For instance, in a group of twenty players, the following names may be used:

la rosa	el médico
la vaca	el árbol
la gallina	la abuelita
la ventana	el bisabuelo
la cama	el carro
la profesora	la niña
el caballo	el avión
el trigo	la nube
el camino	el presidente
el jardín	la reina

The leader says: *Al cruzar el camino vi la gallina leyendo el periódico.* The player with the name of *gallina* replies: *Se equivoca Ud., yo hablaba con el caballo.* The horse says: *Te equivocas tú, yo dormía.* If no other name is mentioned in the reply, the leader could say: *Al pasar por la ventana vi la rosa.* The rose says: *Se equivoca Ud., yo estaba en el jardín.* The garden says: *Te equivocas tú, yo no tengo rosas en este tiempo.*

If a player makes a mistake, he or she must drop out of the game or suffer whatever penalty was established at the beginning of the game. The winner is the last player left.

16. *Porque quiero a mi novio(a)*

It is very interesting to play this game with students who have an extensive vocabulary in Spanish. It may also be used with first-year students.

A letter of the alphabet is given to each player; the player will use words beginning with that letter to tell why he or she is fond of a boy or a girl. For instance, the one assigned the letter *a* may say: *Quiero a mi novia porque se llama Amalia; porque siempre habla alto; porque vive en la Argentina; porque siempre es amable; porque le gusta el azul.* The one assigned *b* may say: *Quiero a mi novio porque juega al béisbol; porque es bueno; porque me dio un beso; porque es bondadoso; porque viene de Bolivia.* All the letters of the Spanish alphabet except *x* may be used. If a small group is playing, it is a good idea to make a selection of the most important letters. If the group is large, more than one letter could be used for each player.

Keen competition could develop with this game. Perhaps three advanced students, or three "A" students, could serve as judges. Awards or prizes are always a motivation for improvement.

17. *Palabras compuestas*

The objective of this game is to develop skills in recognizing complex words made up of more than one simple word.

The leader writes a list of long words on the board, using a dictionary as reference. From the long word, the players must make as many shorter Spanish words as possible. For example, *Santiguamiento* contains the vowels *a, e, i, o, u,* and the consonants *s, n, t, g,* and *m.* From that word the following can be obtained: *sigo, suma, sana, sano, santa, sitio, Santiago, mientes, santiguo.* The winner of the game is the one with the longest list of correct Spanish words. No repetitions are permissible.

7

Typical Costumes

Each Spanish-speaking country has a variety of regional costumes. It is difficult, therefore, to describe a "typical" costume for each country. This chapter will cover only a few. The Spanish Club can use this material as a guide for making costumes to be used in club activities.

Argentina

The *gaucho* is the symbol of the Argentine *pampas*, and his costume goes with that tradition. The gaucho costumes are frequently used when groups get together for native folk dances and songs, and during festivals and national holidays.

The traditional gaucho is characterized by the *chiripa*, a woven blanket or a piece of cloth which is held in place at the waist by a wide ornamental belt decorated with silver. The *chiripa* is worn, apronlike, over wide baggy trousers called *bombachos*, which disappear into leather boots that reach far above the knees. A short, embroidered jacket is worn over a loose white shirt, which is finished at the neck with a knotted handkerchief. The gauchos always wear a black felt hat and a long silver-handled knife that goes through the belt; they always carry a riding whip. The gaucho's partner usually dresses with full skirt, a simple white blouse, apron, and scarf.

During celebrations the gauchos and their partners perform such dances as *el gato, la melamba,* and *el pericón. El gato* is performed to the rhythm of guitars. *La melamba* is performed by two gauchos. *El pericón* is the national dance of Argentina and is a group dance.

Bolivia

There are many different Indian villages in Bolivia, each with its own costumes. Red, yellow, purplish red, green, and sky blue are the colors of the *chola*, who is a woman of mixed Spanish and Indian ancestry. She dresses by putting one skirt over the other, sometimes wearing as many as five in different colors. The skirts are accented by high-heeled colored boots and a white blouse under a silk shawl. The chola's hair is worn in several braids that are sometimes adorned with silver ornaments. A small derby either of felt or highly varnished white straw completes her costume and is, in fact, one of the most important pieces.

The clothing of the Aymará Indians who live in Bolivia's high altitudes differs slightly. The men wear a knitted *vicuña* wool cap with long ear tabs to protect them from the cold of the mountains. They often wear a large felt hat over the cap. The Indian's homespun two-piece suit has slit trousers which reveal beneath a strip of white cotton cloth. A woolen *poncho*, or blanket, over the Indian's clothes protects him from rain and cold. The women of the tribe wear heavy woolen blouses and skirts fastened together by wide red woolen girdles. They wear heavy shawls over their clothes and a small felt hat.

Chile

In Chile one of the most beautiful costumes is that of the Araucanians, who are primarily farmers. The women's hair is braided in two smooth braids and the head is wrapped in a cloth like a turban. An indigo blue or black blanket dress is worn over a white blouse; it is belted at the waist and pinned at either shoulder with a round silver pin. Outdoors, a *poncho* woven of *guanaco* is used, and over it a long *ichella*, or shawl, is wrapped. This shawl goes over the shoulders and is fastened at the front with a silver pin. This costume is completed by the woman's silver ornaments which include large earrings, necklaces, and headbands of silver coins. The men wear a loose shirt and the *chiripá* that is very similar to the one worn by the Argentine *gaucho*, over which a black or blue poncho is used.

The costume of the *huaso*, or cowboy of Chile, is similar to that of the *gaucho*, but is more simple. The *huaso* wears boots and spurs, a colored handkerchief, and a hip-length *poncho*. A sharp pointed knife is carried and held in place by a belt. His costume is gracefully displayed especially when the *huaso* dances *la cueca*, which is the national dance of Chile.

Colombia

Colombia has preserved many traditional costumes of Spain. The Colombian women's clothes consist of a simple dress in delicate colors such as: lavender, yellow, or pink. For Sunday Mass, *las señoritas* are seen wearing dresses with shoulder-length *mantillas* which cover their hair. The Indian woman dresses in a white blouse and a dark, full skirt. Over her head she wears a shawl with a straw hat. Many of the Indian men wear conventional clothes covered with a *ruana*. They also wear straw hats.

Costa Rica

Costa Rica does not have a national costume. During holidays and festivals the village people usually wear gala dresses of generations ago. The woman's costume consists of a low-cut blouse, with ruffled or puffed short sleeves and a cotton skirt with flower designs. A brightly colored silk kerchief is knotted at the neck and fastened by a flower. The finishing touch of the costume is a light and delicate silk shawl in a deep bright color. Her hair is braided with ribbon bands and a flower over the left ear.

The typical man's costume consists of a white shirt, white or dark trousers, a silk kerchief, and a band worn around the waist and knotted on the right side. A straw hat and a dark jacket complete the outfit. Sunday afternoons are for the family, who enjoy being together, playing *la guitarra* and *el tamborcito,* and dancing the *zapaceados* and the *boleros. La marimba,* Central America's favorite musical instrument, is played at large gatherings and important occasions. It is a percussion instrument similar to the xylophone.

Dominican Republic

The Dominican Republic has few provincial costumes. Ranch owners wear a *sombrero* and a colorful handkerchief. Their wives wear elegant and expensive embroidered shawls and high tortoise-shell combs, as a symbol of their social status. In the rural parts of the Republic, people wear simple shirts and trousers. The women wear long, loose dresses and gold earrings.

Ecuador

The costumes of the Indians in Ecuador differ according to the villages. The Otavalo Indian women have one of the most interesting costumes. They wear tight, dark blue skirts, white blouses, and red woven belts. They carry *rebozos* of different colors and design. If a woman is unmarried, the *rebozo* is folded over her left shoulder. Around the neck, gold and red beads are displayed.

The *poncho* is unique to the Quechua Indians. It protects them against the cold and the wind. The men wear their *ponchos* over white cotton shirts and trousers; the women wear them over blouses and long handwoven skirts. Often a scarf is added for more protection. Both men and women wear large, white felt hats. The man usually carries a *rondador*, which is a little flute.

El Salvador

The Indian women of El Salvador wear a loose, short sleeved dress, with a brightly colored scarf draped over the left shoulder. The skirts and aprons are of various materials and lengths, depending on the village. The Salvadoran *peón* wears white trousers and shirt, a bright scarf around the throat, and a felt hat. Leather soled sandals are used when he goes to town; otherwise he walks barefoot.

Honduras

The Honduran men on the plantation wear loose shirts and trousers, with short, fancy jackets and sandals. Their heads are protected by a combination of kerchief and felt hat. The Honduran woman's costume consists of a loose, white cotton blouse with a low neck and short sleeves; a colored skirt; and a plain apron. A *rebozo* is wrapped around the face and head, and goes around the waist and over the shoulder. The black woman substitutes a bright turban for the *rebozo*.

Mexico

Each state in Mexico has its own beautiful native costume.

The Tehuanas live on the Isthmus of Tehuantepec. The Tehuana woman wears one of the most exquisite costumes. It consists of a short sleeved, low cut red blouse with embroidered designs in different colors.

The *cotón*, or blouse, is similar to the *huepilli* of the Aztec woman, and the skirt is made of bright cotton material. Below the skirt is a beautiful petticoat that floats above the bare ankles and feet. On market days she wears a dark *rebozo* over her head and shoulders. Over her head she carries a hand-painted *jecapezel,* which is made of dried gourd and is gracefully painted, filled with vegetables and fruit. During *fiestas* the *rebozo* is replaced by a white *huipil grande,* a white cotton lace headdress which forms a delicate frame around the face. The cotton blouse is replaced with one of lace or silk. She completes her costume by adding bracelets and necklaces.

Indians of the Yucatan peninsula still wear costumes which indicate their Mayan origins. The Mayan woman's *huipil,* or single sleeveless garment, has beautiful embroidery on the neck, shoulders, and hem. The dress comes to below the knees, under which a lace-edged petticoat falls to the ankles. A neck scarf in bright colors, a few necklaces, and some flowers for the hair add grace to the costume.

The Mexican *peón* wears a white shirt and white or colored trousers; over his clothes he uses a striped *sarape,* or blanket, that protects him from the cold and the wind. A huge straw *sombrero* and sandals complete the costume.

Mexico's national dance, *el jarabe tapatío,* is traditionally performed by a girl dressed in *china poblana* and the man in the *charro,* or Mexican cowboy, costume. These costumes are worn only on holidays, festivals, and other special occasions. The *china poblana* costume consists of a white blouse, a spangled red and green skirt, and high-heeled slippers. A scarf around the neck, strings of beads with ribbons and flowers on her head, and earrings and bracelets add the final touches to this magnificent costume. Her partner, *el charro,* wears tight black trousers which are ornamented on the outer seams with heavy gold or silver embroidery and rows of closely placed gold or silver buttons. The silk shirt he wears is also embroidered and is worn under a short black jacket. A *sarape* is flung carelessly over the shoulder and a scarlet kerchief is tied around the neck. The elegant costume is topped with a huge felt *sombrero,* with gold or silver braid.

During the *jarabe tapatío, el charro* throws his *sombrero* to the ground and *la china poblana* dances around the enormous brim. *El charro* then makes a gesture in submission to his partner; she later holds his *sombrero* behind her head in a symbol of victory. *El son de la negra, Vera Cruz,* and *La sandunga* are other Mexican dances. *La ranchera mariachi* and *música romántica* are the country's favorite kinds of music. The costumes of the *mariachi* are the same as those of *los charros.*

Peru

Peruvian Indians love fiestas, and many of their traditional costumes are worn on those occasions. For the Peruvians the *poncho*, the brimmed hat, and sandals are important pieces of the costume. Under a broad hat, the men wear caps with wide upturned brims made of wool. These caps are decorated with small animal and human figures of early Inca design. In the highlands, the women wear short skirts and, like *las cholas* in Bolivia, they use one skirt on top of another. Over the low-cut blouse the Peruvian woman uses a shawl or *ichella*. These have different purposes; one is to carry a baby on her back. In some areas, women wear a rectangular head-dress that protects them from inclement weather. This blue or red head-dress is carefully ornamented with rhinestones; around the edge it has an overlapping piece of cloth forming a veil that is turned back for further protection from the weather. The costume is topped with a huge blue hat, adorned with rhinestones. The Peruvian woman's headdress changes from village to village. In some places a scarf is worn under the flat, broad-brimmed hat, which is made of homespun wool and trimmed with gold or silver rhinestones. To avoid frostbite, women use strips of wool cloth over their ears and under the hat.

8

Food and Drink

This chapter introduces members to some Hispanic recipes. There is a section with Spanish-English food vocabulary that could be very useful when planning a meal as an activity for the club. Hispanic food is, of course, diverse due to the vast geographical extension of these nations, the products available, and the eating habits developed over the centuries. Each of these countries has its own personality and cuisine. Fish is abundant along the coastal areas of Spain and Latin America. The year-round abundance of fruit distinguishes Latin America and is an indispensable part of its cuisine. Some of the fruit is exported to other continents. The following is a list of some fruit from Latin America that we see every day in the market; delicious dishes can be prepared from them.

1. *Plátanos and guineos*

One of the most popular crops in Latin America is plantains, known as *plátanos* or *guineos*. Plantains are members of the banana family and sometimes grow to be more than a foot long. They can be boiled, fried, or baked. Thin slices of the ripened plantains that are dipped in a batter of egg and bread crumbs and later fried in deep fat make delicious fritters.

2. *Papayas*

Ripe *papayas* are always sweet. They are a common breakfast or after-dinner fruit. Latin Americans eat them with a spoon or knife and fork; they also can be made into puddings, pie, juice, or candy.

3. *Aguacates*

The *aguacate*, or avocado, grows on a fine, shiny-leafed tree and is considered a fruit, although many think of it as a vegetable. It is used in everyday meals and is often eaten raw, either alone or in salads. Mashed avocado with grated onion, lemon juice, and seasoning makes a delicious *guacamole* (see recipe #1). It can also be cooked, baked with shrimp purée and covered with grated cheese.

4. *Piñas*

The pineapples that come to the United States are mostly of inferior varieties that will withstand shipping; they are picked green and sour, ripening at the market or in one's kitchen. In Mexico they are so fragrant that one of them perfumes an entire room, and they are so sweet that no extra sugar is needed. *Piñas* can be made into juice, candy, desserts, salads, or stuffing for chicken and turkey. A cold appetizer can be made by cutting off the top of a large, ripe pineapple and scooping out the pulp and core without touching the skin. The cavity is filled with pieces of lobster and shrimp mixed with mayonnaise, pieces of apple, and pineapple. The top is replaced and the stuffed pineapple served.

5. *Guayabas*

Guava is a fruit which grows wild along the roadsides of many Latin American countries. A guava is a yellow fruit about the size of a plum, with a layer of flesh, usually deep pink, surrounding a central cavity full of pulp and small, hard seeds. The fruit is eaten as it comes from the tree or made into a dark-red paste or used for juice. The paste is usually accompanied by white cheese made from goat's or cow's milk.

6. *Granadillas*

Passion fruit, *granadilla*, is a deep red fruit, slightly bigger than a hen's egg. The fruit is easily broken in two; the interior is packed with small seeds, each one encased in a delicate covering. Granadillas can be eaten raw or squeezed to make juice.

Other fruit that seldom reaches the United States includes: *sapote* from Mexico, *sapodilla* from Peru, *lucuma* from Peru and Chile, *chirimoya* from Peru, and *jacá* from Venezuela.

Recipes

The following recipes originated in several Latin American countries and in Spain. Some can be prepared at Spanish Club activities, while others must be prepared at home. They can be an integral part of special Club celebrations, especially those to which nonmembers have been invited. These recipes are, in fact, a delicious way to introduce others to Hispanic culture.

1. Guacamole (Mexico)

2 large ripe avocados
2 small tomatoes, peeled, seeded, and chopped
2 tablespoons of chopped onion
1 tablespoon of chopped fresh coriander *(cilantro)*

1 tablespoon of rinsed and chopped canned chili *(serrano)*
½ teaspoon salt
⅛ teaspoon freshly ground black pepper

Cut the avocados in half. Remove the seed and any brown or black spots. With a spoon, detach and remove the pulp from the skin. In a large mixing bowl, mash the pulp with a fork until it reaches a purée consistency. Add the chopped onion, chili, tomatoes, coriander, salt, and black pepper. Mix all the ingredients gently. Taste for seasoning. To prevent the *guacamole* from darkening, add a few drops of lime and mix, or cover it with a plastic wrap and refrigerate until ready to use. Stir before serving.

Guacamole is served as a dip with fried tortillas, as a sauce for tacos or *tostadas*, or as a salad on top of crispy lettuce. It is also good as a side dish.

2. Frijoles refritos (Mexico)

2 cups dried pink beans
1 cup chopped onions
6 cups cold water
2 medium tomatoes, peeled and seeded
1 teaspoon crumbled and seeded dried chili
½ teaspoon finely chopped garlic

¼ teaspoon crumbled *epazote*, if available
¼ teaspoon freshly ground black pepper
½ cup lard
1 teaspoon salt

Clean the beans by running cold water over them for five minutes until water over them for five minutes until the water runs clean. Discard any black or shriveled beans. In a heavy pot combine the water, ½ cup of the chopped onions, ¼ cup of the tomatoes, ¼ teaspoon of the garlic, the chili, *epazote,* and the pepper. Bring the water to a boil over high heat, add the beans, reduce to medium heat, and half-cover the pan. Simmer at medium heat for 30 minutes. Check to see if the beans are tender; if not, cook for 15 more minutes. During the cooking time stir the beans gently every 20 minutes to prevent their sticking to the bottom of the pan. Remove the pan from the heat, and cover it to keep the beans warm.

In a 12-inch skillet, melt 2 tablespoons of lard over medium heat until a light haze forms above it. Add the remaining onions and garlic, lower the heat, and fry for about 5 minutes, or until the onions are transparent but not brown. Stir in the remaining tomatoes and simmer for 3 minutes. Fry the cooled beans as follows: Add 3 tablespoons of the beans to the pan of simmering sauce, mash them with a fork, and stir in one tablespoon of the remaining lard. Continue to add and mash the beans, following each addition with a tablespoon of lard until all the beans and lard have been used. Cook over low heat for 10 minutes, stirring frequently until the beans are dry. When it is time to serve, transfer the beans to a bowl or dish. This dish is the traditional companion to tortilla dishes and main courses; it is also a dip.

Note: Be careful when working with chiles. Use gloves when cleaning them. Wash your hands with soap and water after handling hot chiles of any kind. Wash the chiles in cold water to remove the seeds.

3. *Papas a la huancaina (Peru)*

1 large onion, peeled and cut in rings
8 medium potatoes, peeled
¼ cup fresh lemon juice
1½ teaspoons crumbled, seeded dried *hontaka* chili or 3 *pequin* chiles
ground black pepper
1 teaspoon salt
1 cup coarsely crumbled *queso blanco* or fresh mozzarella cheese
⅔ cup heavy cream

1 teaspoon turmeric
2 teaspoons finely chopped and seeded fresh red or green hot chili
⅓ cup olive oil
4 hard cooked eggs, cut into halves
8 black olives
lettuce leaves
1 fresh red or green hot chili, stemmed, seeded, and cut into strips

Put the potatoes into a large pan of lightly salted boiling water, and boil them until tender but not overcooked. Drain the water and set the potatoes aside. In a large bowl, combine the lemon juice, the 1½ teaspoons of dried chili, ½ teaspoon of salt, and a dash of black pepper. Add the onion rings. Mix all the ingredients so that the onions are evenly covered with the mixture. Cover the bowl and set aside to marinate at room temperature.

To make the sauce combine in a blender the cheese, cream, turmeric, chopped fresh chili, ½ teaspoon salt, and a few dashes of pepper. Blend at high speed until creamy. In a skillet, heat the olive oil over medium heat. Pour in the cheese and cream sauce, reduce the heat to low, and cook for 10 minutes, stirring constantly, until it reaches a thick consistency.

To serve, arrange the potatoes on a heated platter and pour the sauce over them. Drain the onion rings and put them over the potatoes with the chili strips. Garnish with eggs, black olives and crispy lettuce.

4. Escabeche de gallina (Chile)

⅓ cup olive oil
4 pounds of chicken, cut for
   6 or 8 servings
1 cup dry white vinegar
1 cup hot water
3 medium onions, peeled
   and diced
2 carrots, scraped and cut
   diagonally into slices
1 small leek cut in slices

1 tablespoon salt
1 celery top, 2 parsley sprigs,
   2 bay leaves, 2 whole cloves
   and ¼ teaspoon thyme
   wrapped together in
   cheesecloth to make a
   bouquet garni
1 lemon, cut lengthwise into
   halves and then crosswise
   into slices

In a large casserole, heat the olive oil at medium heat. Dry the chicken with paper towels and add it to the casserole to brown in the oil, a few pieces at a time. Add all the ingredients including the bouquet garni, and bring to a boil over high heat. Reduce the heat to low. Cover and simmer undisturbed for 30 minutes, or until the chicken is tender but not overcooked. Remove the bouquet garni, and arrange the chicken pieces in one layer in a deep serving dish. Pour the cooking liquid with the vegetables over the chicken. Decorate the top with lemon slices, and cool at room temperature. Cover the dish and refrigerate for at least 6 hours, or until the liquids have jelled. Serve on chilled plates as a main course.

5. *Huevos revueltos flamencos (Spain)*

3 medium potatoes
¼ cup olive oil
2 tablespoons butter
1 small white onion, finely
  chopped
½ medium pepper, chopped
½ cup minced ham

1 whole pimiento, chopped
2 tablespoons tomato sauce
6 eggs
1 tablespoon vanilla
  dash hot sauce
½ cup chopped toasted
  almonds

Peel and cut the potatoes in small pieces. Cook them in salted water until soft but firm. Keep the potatoes in the water until ready to use. Heat the oil and butter, and add the onion and pepper. Sautée until transparent but not brown. Drain the potatoes, add them to the onions and pepper and cook until golden. Add the ham, pimiento, and tomato sauce; cover the pan and cook over low heat for 10 minutes.

Meanwhile, beat the eggs with the vanilla and the hot sauce until light. Pour the mixture in the pan and mix in gently in a folding motion until the eggs are set but not dry. Serve and sprinkle with toasted almonds.

6. *Huevos a la cubana*

1 cup olive oil (or vegetable oil)
1 garlic clove, crushed

12 eggs (2 per person)
2 ripe plantains

Heat the oil in a skillet with the crushed garlic clove. When the garlic is completely brown, but not burned, discard. Break 2 eggs into a saucer. Slide into the hot oil and spoon hot oil over the eggs until cooked to your taste, but do not turn the eggs.

Lift eggs from the oil with a slotted spoon, draining as much oil as possible. Arrange them on a heated platter. Fry the rest of the eggs the same way. Place platter in a warm oven. Peel 2 plantains and slice them at an angle. Fry the slices in the same skillet where the eggs were fried, adding more oil if necessary. After they have fried to a golden brown, drain them on paper towels, and serve with the eggs.

Huevos a la cubana are usually served with rice and avocado.

7. *Caldo de pollo (Latin America)*

1 stewing hen (3–4 pounds)	1 small potato
1 medium onion	½ medium green pepper
2 crisp celery stalks, cut in two	2 bay leaves
1 garlic clove, crushed	1 tablespoon salt
2 medium ripe whole tomatoes	

Use a soup kettle or Dutch oven with cover. Place the entire hen in the pot. Add all the ingredients. Fill the pot three-quarters full of water. Bring to a rapid boil and skim several times to ensure a clear broth. Lower heat, cover, and cook slowly until hen is tender and begins to fall apart. If necessary, add more water to make at least 2 quarts of broth.

When the cooking time is up, let it cool completely. Set it aside for 3 hours, strain and use for soups or in preparation of dishes. This *caldo* can also be served warm.

8. *Chayote relleno (Mexico)*

3 large *chayotes*	1 cup sugar
3 eggs, lightly beaten	4 cups finely crumbled pound cake
¾ cup sweet grape juice	
1½ teaspoon ground nutmeg	½ cup slivered blanched almonds
1 cup seedless raisins	

Preheat the oven to 350°F. Cut the *chayotes* in half lengthwise and place them in a medium saucepan. Cover them with cold water, and bring to a boil over medium heat. Reduce the heat to low, cover the pan and simmer for 30 minutes, or until the *chayotes* show no resistance when pierced with the tip of a sharp knife. Drain the *chayotes*. When cool enough to handle, remove the seeds with a small spoon. Then scoop out the pulp, leaving a thin pulp layer intact inside the shell. In a large bowl, mash the pulp with a fork until it is perfectly smooth. Then gradually beat in the eggs, grape juice, and ground nutmeg. Add the raisins, sugar, and cake, and beat again. The filling should have the consistency of mashed potatoes and should hold its shape in a spoon; add more crumbs if needed. Fill each *chayote* shell with the filling, smooth the top, and dot with almonds. Arrange the shells side by side in a buttered baking dish and bake for 15 minutes, or until the top of the filling is golden.

9. Chicharrones de pollo (Dominican Republic)

1½ teaspoons dark vinegar
¼ cup soy sauce
¼ cup strained fresh lime juice
4 pounds chicken, cut in 16
    small pieces

2 cups vegetable oil
½ teaspoon salt
½ teaspoon black pepper
1 cup flour

Add the soy sauce and lime juice to the vinegar. Place the chicken in a deep bowl and pour in the vinegar mixture, turning the pieces with a spoon to coat them evenly. Marinate at room temperature for about 2 hours, or in the refrigerator for at least 6 hours, turning the pieces occasionally. In a 12-inch skillet, heat the oil over high heat until it is very hot but not smoking. Pat the pieces of chicken completely dry with paper towels and season them with salt and pepper. Dip them in the flour, and fry 5 pieces of chicken at a time for about 6 minutes on each side. Turn the pieces and regulate the heat so they color evenly without burning. When they have a deep gold color, transfer the pieces to the baking dish and keep them warm in the oven, which has been previously heated at a low setting.

Serve the chicken warm accompanied with yellow or white rice and beans or frijoles.

10. Natillas piuranas (Latin America)

1 can condensed milk
    (15 ounces)
3 cups fresh milk

¼ cup water
1 cup dark-brown sugar
½ teaspoon cornstarch

In a small pot, mix the condensed milk, fresh milk, and cornstarch; bring to a boil, stirring constantly. Remove from heat. Combine the sugar and water in a medium saucepan, stir and cook over low heat until the sugar dissolves. Pour in the hot milk and stir well. Cook on low heat for 1 hour and 15 minutes, stirring a few times. The mixture will change to a thick amber-colored pudding. Serve the pudding at room temperature or refrigerate it and serve it chilled.

11. *Moros y cristianos (Cuba)*

3 cups cool water
1 cup black beans
1 small onion
1 bay leaf
1 small ripe tomato
1 tablespoon salt
¼ cup olive oil
½ pound lean pork
¼ pound diced cooked ham

1 medium onion, finely
    chopped
½ medium green pepper
1 garlic clove, minced
1 teaspoon crushed oregano
    salt and hot sauce to taste
1½ cups raw long grain rice
1 tablespoon lemon juice

Wash beans over cool water until the water runs clear; discard any foreign particles or damaged beans. Pour the 3 cups of water in a pan and add the beans. Cover the pan and leave it overnight.

Next day, pour the water and beans into a soup kettle. Add the whole peeled onion, bay leaf, and whole tomato. Add water, if necessary, to cover beans 1 inch above. Bring to a rapid boil, cover; lower heat and cook until beans are soft. Use only a wooden spoon to stir the beans. When beans are cooked, add 1 tablespoon of salt and cook 5 minutes longer. Drain the beans and measure the liquid. If liquid does not measure 2½ cups, add water to the correct amount. Discard whatever is left of the onion, whole tomato, and bay leaf. Reserve beans and liquid for later use.

Heat ¼ cup oil in deep skillet. Add the pork and brown on moderate heat. Lower heat, cover, and cook 15 minutes. Combine ham, onion, pepper, minced garlic, and oregano and add to the skillet. Mix and sautée until onion and pepper are very soft. Add salt and hot sauce to taste. Add the rice and fry gently with the sautéed ingredients for about 10 minutes, stirring to mix well. Add lemon juice, beans, and the 2½ cups of liquid. Bring to a boil; stir once, cover and place in preheated 325°F oven for 20 minutes. Remove from oven. Cover and allow to stand 15 minutes before serving.

12. *Pudin de fruta (Spain)*

6 tablespoons sugar
5 slices bread, crust trimmed
2 cups milk
5 whole eggs
5 tablespoons sugar
¼ teaspoon salt
1 teaspoon vanilla

1 can (8 ounces) fruit cocktail
¼ cup seedless raisins
6 maraschino cherries,
    chopped
½ cup finely chopped pecans
8 thin slices guava paste

Caramelize the 6 tablespoons of sugar in a skillet over low heat and quickly coat bottom of a glass baking dish. (The sugar is caramelized when it is totally dissolved and turns a dark amber color. Work quickly with it so that it doesn't burn.)

Cube bread and place in a deep bowl. Add the 2 cups of milk. Beat eggs with the sugar, salt, and vanilla. Add to bread mixture in bowl. Mix well and set aside for ½ hour. Crumble bread with fork during soaking period.

Add fruit cocktail, seedless raisins, cherries, and the pecans to the bread mixture. Mix well and pour into prepared baking dish. Place baking dish in a double boiler *(al baño de María)* and bake for about 50 minutes at 350°F. Cool, then invert onto a suitable serving dish, deep enough so that it will hold the sauce as it drips down the sides of the pudding. Allow to cool completely before cutting into squares.

This dish is an excellent dessert for parties.

13. *Torta (Spain)*

8 egg whites	8 egg yolks
16 tablespoons sugar	1 teaspoon lemon juice
8 tablespoons all-purpose flour	1 teaspoon grated lemon peel

Preheat the oven to 350°F. Beat egg whites until soft peaks form. Gradually add sugar and continue beating until the mixture has the consistency of meringue. Add the flour all at once over the mix. Fold in and blend well but gently. Beat egg yolks lightly with the lemon juice and peel. Fold into egg white-flour mixture carefully (do not beat). Pour the mixture into an angel cake pan and bake at 350°F oven for 30 minutes, or until a toothpick inserted in cake comes out clean. Wait until cool (about 35 minutes) and invert the pan over a plate.

14. *Polvorones (Latin America)*

½ pound butter	1 teaspoon baking powder
1 cup granulated sugar	½ teaspoon salt
½ cup confectioners' sugar	1 teaspoon vanilla
2 eggs	½ cup sugar
4 cups all-purpose flour, sifted	1 teaspoon cinnamon

Preheat oven to 375°F. Cream butter with the granulated and confectioners' sugar until very creamy and light. Add baking powder and salt to the flour and then add the flour to the cream mixture, a third at a time. Blend in the vanilla. Roll out on floured board to about ¼-inch thickness. Cut with round cookie cutter or make a small ball in the palm of your hand. Place on greased cookie sheet about 1 inch apart and bake for approximately 12 minutes, or until light gold in color. Sprinkle with a mixture of sugar and cinnamon while still hot.

15. *Refresco de coco y piña (Dominican Republic)*

2 cups coconut milk, made of fresh coconut	2 tablespoons sugar
	almond or vanilla extract
2½ cups chopped fresh pineapple	

Combine the coconut milk, pineapple, and sugar in a blender and mix at high speed for 30 seconds. Pour the entire contents into a strainer set over a deep bowl and lined with a double thickness of cheesecloth. Press down hard over the pineapple with the back of a spoon to extract all its juices before discarding the pulp.

Taste the *refresco* and add more sugar and a drop or two of vanilla or almond extract if desired. Cover and refrigerate for at least 2 hours or until chilled.

Note: To make the coconut milk, cut the coconut in half and use a knife to separate the pulp from the shell. Cut it in small pieces, pour into a blender with two cups of hot water and purée. Pour the mixture through a strainer to obtain the milk.

16. *Sangría (Spain)*

¾ cup fresh lime juice	3 cups of water
1½ cups sugar	ice
1¼ cups grape juice	

Mix all the ingredients and serve chilled.

17. Té de jengibre (Latin America)

1 cup water   1 teaspoon sugar
1 piece of mashed ginger

Wash, crush, and add the ginger with the cup of water to a saucepan. Bring it to a boil over medium heat. Add sugar. Keep mixture in a covered teapot to preserve the flavor until ready to serve.

18. Ponche (Latin America)

1 egg white   3 tablespoons pineapple juice
⅓ cup powdered sugar   6 ounces light club soda
6 maraschino cherries   1 can concentrated lime juice
3 tablespoons cherry juice   (6 ounces)
⅓ cup crushed pineapple

Fill a blender container three-quarters full of crushed ice. Add ingredients in the order listed and blend at high speed until foamy. Serve.

19. Ponche tropical (Spain)

2 quarts ginger ale   2 ounces coconut syrup
1 can unsweetened pineapple   1 cup fresh lime juice
   juice   4 scoops of lime sherbet
1 8-ounce jar maraschino   mint leaves
   cherries with stems,
   well drained

Have all ingredients chilled. Use a deep pot for mixing. In the center of the bowl place a small block of ice. Combine all ingredients in the mixing pot and pour over the ice as needed.

20. *Coquí (Latin America)*

1 cup coconut cream	1 teaspoon vanilla extract
(*Coco López*)	½ cup condensed milk
¾ cup evaporated milk	1 teaspoon cinnamon
2 egg yolks	freshly grated nutmeg

Combine the coconut cream, evaporated milk, condensed milk, egg yolks and vanilla in a blender, and blend at high speed for 30 seconds, or until the mixture is smooth. Add the cinnamon and blend for a few more seconds. Refrigerate the *coquí* into chilled parfait or punch glasses and sprinkle the top lightly with nutmeg.

9

Vocabulary for Spanish Menus

1. ### *Appetizers*

    oysters
    olives
    pickled fish
    shrimp
    smoked salmon
    marinated olives

    ### *Aperitivos*

    ostras
    aceitunas
    pescado en escabeche
    camarones (gambas in Spain)
    salmón ahumado
    aceitunas adobadas

2. ### *Soups*

    chicken rice soup
    avocado cream soup
    chicken soup
    fish soup
    vegetable soup
    chicken broth
    beef stock
    garlic soup
    tomato soup
    Spanish chick-pea soup
    vermicelli soup

    ### *Sopas*

    sopa de pollo y arroz
    sopa de crema de aguacate
    sopa de pollo
    sopa de pescado
    sopa de vegetales
    caldo de pollo
    clado de res
    sopa de ajo
    crema de tomate
    sopa de garbanzos
    sopa de fideos

3. ### *Salads*   *Ensaladas*

shrimp salad	ensalada de camarones (gambas)
lettuce salad	ensalada de lechuga
lobster salad	ensalada de langosta
coleslaw and tomatoes	repollo y tomates
seafood salad	ensalada de mariscos
tropical fruit salad	ensalada de frutas
asparagus salad	ensalada de espárragos
cactus leaf salad	ensalada de hojas de cactus

4. ### *Salad dressings*   *Aderezo para ensaladas*

oil and vinegar	aceite y vinagre
parsley dressing	aderezo de perejil
homemade mayonnaise	mayonesa casera
lemon dressing	aderezo de limón
anchovy dressing	aderezo de anchoas
roquefort dressing	aderezo de queso roquefort

5. ### *Fish*   *Pescado*

trout	trucha
herring	arenque
salmon	salmón
sole	lenguado
codfish	bacalao
squid	calamares
tuna fish	atún
sardines	sardinas

6. ### *Poultry*   *Aves*

duck	pato
chicken	pollo
turkey	pavo
squab	pichón
goose	ganso
partridge	perdiz

7.	**Meat**	**Carne**
	roast	asado
	fried sausage	salchicha frita
	pickled pork	cerdo en escabeche
	fillet	filete
	veal	ternera
	chicken fricassee	fricasé de pollo
	lamb	cordero
	liver	hígado
	beef stew	guisado de carne
	cooked ham	jamón cocido
	bacon	tocino
	beef	carne de res

8.	**Sauces**	**Salsas**
	annatto oil	aceite de achiote
	Argentine spiced	salsa argentina picante
	Chilean hot sauce	salsa chilena picante
	green tomato sauce	salsa verde de tomate
	pepper and lemon sauce	salsa de pimienta y limón
	red chili sauce	salsa roja de chile
	spicy avocado sauce	salsa picante de aguacate

9.	**Vegetables**	**Vegetales**
	mushrooms	hongos (champiñones)
	green beans	habichuelas (judías) verdes
	cucumbers	pepinillos (pepinos)
	carrots	zanahorias
	red cabbage	repollo morado
	white cabbage	repollo blanco
	asparagus	espárrago
	ginger	jengibre
	eggplant	berenjena
	peppers	pimientos
	pumpkin	calabaza
	onion	cebolla
	garlic	ajo

10.

Egg dishes	*Platos con huevos*
boiled eggs	huevos cocidos
scrambled eggs	huevos revueltos
fried eggs	huevos fritos
poached eggs	huevos escalfados
omelets	tortillas
rice omelet	tortilla de arroz
eggs in a nest	huevos al nido
Spanish omelet	tortilla española
country-style omelet	tortilla campesina
ranch-style eggs	huevos rancheros
eggs Cuban style	huevos a la cubana
scrambled eggs with cheese	revoltillo de huevo de queso
and parsley	y perejil

11.

Side dishes	*"acompañado con"*
fried potatoes	papas (patatas) fritas
mashed potatoes	puré de papas (patatas)
white rice	arroz blanco
yellow rice	arroz amarillo
beans	habichuelas (frijoles; judías)
salad	ensalada
fried plantains	plátanos fritos

12.

Preparation	*Preparación*
roast/fried	asado/frito
baked	al horno
stuffed	relleno
boiled	cocido
with: butter	con: mantequilla
honey	miel
pepper	pimientos
cream	crema
salt	sal
mustard	mostaza
gravy	salsa
catsup	salsa de tomate

sugar	azúcar
sweet potatoes	batatas
raw	crudo
grilled	a la parrilla
in sauce	en salsa
in casserole	a la caserola

13. *Bread and baked goods* — *Pastelería*

cake	torta
cookies	galletas dulces
corn bread	pan de maíz
banana bread	pan de guineos
apple cake	torta de manzana
turnovers	pastelillos (empanadas)
toast	tostadas
garlic bread	pan de ajo
bread	pan

14. *Desserts* — *Postres*

ice cream	helado
fresh fruit	fruta fresca
pudding	pudín
chocolate ice cream	helado de chocolate
coconut ice cream	helado de coco
pineapple custard	flan de piña
custard	flan
guava pie	pastelillo de guayaba
fruit pudding	pudín de fruta
Spanish doughnut	churros
chocolate custard	flan de chocolate
coconut cupcakes	tortitas de coco
pumpkin pudding	pudín de calabaza
royal eggs	huevos reales
thousand-leaf pastry	pastelitos de mil hojas
honey squash	chayote relleno

15. **Beverages**

Beverages	Bebidas
apple juice	jugo de manzana
coffee	café
milk	leche
lemonade	limonada
tea	té
orange juice	jugo de naranja (china)
water	agua
sparkling water	agua de soda
chocolate	chocolate
guava juice	jugo de guayaba
soft drink	soda (refresco)
milk shake	batida
pineapple juice	jugo de piña
apricot juice	jugo de albaricoque
wine	vino
beer	cerveza

16. **Main dishes**

Baked meat-filled turnovers (Argentina)
Baked pumpkin with beef and vegetables (Argentina)
Braised fresh ham with chili sauce (Chile)
Ground beef with apples, olives, and almonds (Mexico)
Lamb and vegetable stew (Chile)
Pork in orange and lemon sauce (Peru)
Chicken and rice stew (Puerto Rico)
Chicken with pineapple (Cuba)
Marinated fried chicken (Dominican Republic)
Roast stuffed duck with pineapple (Dominican Republic)
Kidney stew (Puerto Rico)
Spiced boiled beef with olives and raisins (Cuba)
Eggs Cuban style (Cuba)
Paella (Cuba)
Lamb stew with capers (Spain)
Roast leg of lamb (Latin America)
Stuffed veal chops (Latin America)
Chicken in onion sauce (Latin America)
White rice and black beans sautéed (Cuba)
Spanish omelet (Spain)
Codfish vizcaína (Spain)

Platos principales

Empanadas asadas rellenas de carne (Argentina)
Calabaza al horno con carne y vegetales (Argentina)
Jamón fresco al carbón con salsa de chili (Chile)
Picadillo con manzanas, aceitunas y almendras (México)
Guisado de cordero y vegetales (Chile)
Cerdo en salsa de limón y naranja (Perú)
Asopao de pollo con arroz (Puerto Rico)
Pollo con piña (Cuba)
Pollo frito en escabeche (República Dominicana)
Pato asado relleno de piña (República Dominicana)
Cocido de riñones (Puerto Rico)
Carne picante cocida con aceitunas y pasas (Cuba)
Huevos a la cubana (Cuba)
Paella Valenciana (España)
Coldero estofado con alcaparras (España)
Pierna de cordero asada (América Latina)
Chuletas de ternera rellena (América Latina)
Pollo encebollado (América Latina)
Moros y cristianos (Cuba)
Tortilla española (España)
Bacalao a la vizcaína (España)

10

Spanish Expressions

Colloquialisms, slang, proverbs, and idioms are expressions that are misunderstood by most foreigners. These expressions are often neglected in a formal Spanish curriculum. However, their use will acquaint the club members with the language as it is spoken *en la calle* by native speakers.

This chapter will introduce some regional expressions and reinforce others used throughout the Spanish-speaking world. There is also a useful list of business terms.

1. The following list of expressions can be used in speaking and reading activities.

A continuación—Below; as follows

A la larga—In the long run

Al pie de la letra—Word for word; exactly

A más no poder—To the limit

A mediados de—About the middle of

A ver—Let's see

¡Con razón!—No wonder!

Cueste lo que cueste—Regardless of the cost

Dar tiempo al tiempo—To bide one's time

De buena gana—Willingly; gladly

¡De ninguna manera!—I should say not!

Dicho y hecho—Sure enough; as was expected

¡Eso es!—That's it!; That's right!

Ir a medias—To go 50-50; Dutch treat

No cabe duda—There's no question, or doubt

Pedir prestado—To borrow

Poner al corriente—To keep up-to-date; to inform

¿Puedo servirle en algo?—May I help you?

Sin ton ni son—Without rhyme or reason

Tener prisa—To be in a hurry

2. The following list contains idioms that are used throughout the Spanish-speaking world.

A troche y moche—In confusion and hurry

Andar(se) con rodeos—To beat around the bush

Buscar(le) cinco patas al gato—To look for trouble

Correr a rienda suelta—To run full speed; to run wild

Dar la lata—To bore to death (with a lot of talk)

Dejarlo plantado—To stand one up (on a date or appointment)

Echar flores—To flatter, or compliment

Estirar la pata—To kick the bucket; to kick off; to die

Hacérsele agua la boca—To make one's mouth water (in anticipation)

Ir al grano—To get down to business; to get down to brass tacks

Llover a cántaros—To pour; to rain cats and dogs

Meterse en un lío—To get oneself in a jam

No tener pelos en la lengua—To speak one's mind freely; to be outspoken

Perder los estribos—To loose control of oneself; to go to pieces

Ponerlo a raya—To put one in his (her) place; to hold one in check

Saber al dedillo—To know perfectly

Sacarlo de quicio—To try one's patience; to exasperate one beyond words

Tenerlos entre ojos—To have taken a dislike to one; to have a grudge against one

Tomarle el pelo—To pull one's leg; to kid

Ver la paja en el ojo ajeno—To see other people's faults but fail to see one's own

3. The following are familiar expressions used by Spanish-speaking people.

A las mil maravillas—Wonderfully well; like a million dollars

¡A otro perro con ese hueso!—Tell it to the marines!

¡Así es la vida!—Such is life!

En todas partes se cuecen habas—That can happen anywhere; it happens in the best of families

Eso es harina de otro costal—That's a horse of another color

Lo mismo da—It all adds up to the same thing

No viene al caso—That's not the point

Qué hubo?—What's up?

Qué tal?—How goes it?

¡Son cosas de la vida!—Such is life!

Todo el santo día—All the livelong day; all the blessed day

¡Trato hecho!—It's a deal!

¡Váyase con la música a otra parte!—Go peddle your fish someplace else!

Vivito y coleando—Going strong; alive and kicking

¡Ya lo creo!—Yes, indeed!; I should say so!

4. The following is a list of idioms, expressions, colloquialisms, and slang from different parts of the Spanish-speaking world.

Argentina

Comer de arriba—To be a moocher
Estar en cana—To be in jail
Hacerle la pera—To stand one up (on a date or an appointment)
Pasar el fardo—To pass the buck
Sobre el pucho—Without hesitation

Costa Rica

Comer cuento—To take it all in
Darle atoillo con el dedo—To kid
Estar en la jeruza—To be in the jug, or jail
Hacerse el chango—To play dumb
¡Tumbe la vara!—Don't keep bothering me with that!

Bolivia

Perder soga y cabrito—To play hooky
Hacer la cimarra—To play hooky
Levantarse el larro—To talk a lot about oneself; to praise oneself a lot
Se armó la rosca—All hell broke loose

Cuba

¡Ni de jarana!—I wouldn't dream of it!
Se formó un titingó—All hell broke loose!
Tirarse un papelazo—To make oneself ridiculous

Colombia

Amanecerá y veremos—Time will tell; we'll see
Hacerse el inglés (or gringo)—To play dumb
Ponerle bolas—To be attentive to one; to give one a tumble
Ponerse la leva—To play hooky

Ecuador

Armar boche—To start a fight; to start trouble
Estar empavado—To be out of sorts
Hacerle chino—To fool one
Por la muerte de un judío—Once in a blue moon

El Salvador

Hacerse el papo—To play dumb

Liar el petate—To kick the bucket; to kick off; to die

No pasarlo ni envuelto en huevo—Not to be able to stand one (someone)

Sentirse como pollo comprado—To feel out of place

Tener cuello—To have a lot of pull or influence

Mexico

¡Con dinero baila el chango!—Money talks!

Hacer a uno de chivo los tamales—To double-cross

¡La vida no vale tres cacahuates!—Life isn't worth a darn!; Life isn't worth living!

¡Pícale!—Step on it!; Hurry up!

Ya ni llorar es bueno—Don't cry over spilled milk!

Guatemala

Hacerse el peje—To play dumb

Hacerse el sapo—To play dumb

No pasarlo ni con tragos de agua brasa—Not to be able to stand one (someone)

Patear la cubeta—To kick the bucket; to die

Quedarse sin el mico y sin la montera—To lose everything; to be left with nothing

Nicaragua

Hacer de una aguja un machete—To make a mountain out of a molehill

Pelar el ajo—To kick the bucket; to die

Quedarse sin Beatriz y sin retrato—To lose everything; to be left with nothing

Quedarse viendo para el icaco—To be stood up

Sentirse como gallina comprada—To feel out of place

Honduras

Caerle como píldora—To give one a pain in the neck

¡Hay pericos en la montaña!—The coast is not clear!

Quedarse compuesta y sin novio—To be stood up

Quedarse sin el plato y sin la cena—To lose everything; to be left with nothing

Tener golilla—To have pull, or influence

Panama

¡Cógelo suave!—Take it easy!

Ganarse un camarón—To make a little extra money on the side

Hacer la "ere"—To play hooky

Ponerle el canasto—To pass the buck

Tener olor a leche—To be very young; to be still a baby

Peru

¡A otro burro con esa carga!—Give it to somebody else!

Comerse un pavo—To blush

Pedir el sol por salir—To ask the impossible; to ask for an awful lot

Sobarle la pantorrilla—To polish the apple; to play up to one (someone)

Verle las orejas al galgo—Not to have enough to eat (in the sense of poverty)

Uruguay

Hacerlo largar el hueso—To make one confess

Hacerse la pelada—To play hooky

Tirársela de perro lanudo—To brag, or to go around trying to give the impression that you have more than you really do; that you are better off than you really are

Venezuela

Agarrarlo con el queso en la mano—To catch one red-handed; to catch one with the goods

Estar en la carraplana—To be in a tough spot

Gastar pólvora en zamuros—To waste one's ammunition or efforts on something not worthwhile

Más es la bulla que la cabulla—Much ado about nothing

Business Idioms and Phrases

A la mayor brevedad posible—At one's earliest convenience

A quien corresponda—To whom it may concern

A vuelta de correo—By return mail

Acusar recibo de—To acknowledge receipt of

Al contado—On a cash basis

A crédito—On credit

Con carácter urgente—Rush

Dar anticipadas gracias—To thank in advance

Llegar a nuestro poder—To reach us

Poner en (su) conocimiento—To inform (you)

Por paquete postal—By parcel post

Tener a la vista—To have before one; to have received

Por separado—Under separate cover

Surtir un pedido—To fill an order

Tenemos en nuestro poder—We are in receipt of

Tengo en mi poder—I am in receipt of

Appendix

Addresses for Hispanic Materials

1. *Hispanic Organizations*

The following are useful sources of information and materials.

American Association of Teachers of Spanish and Portuguese (AATSP)
University of Mississippi
University, MS 38655

For teachers of Spanish and Portuguese and literatures related to those languages as well as for anyone interested in Hispanic culture. Operates placement bureau and maintains pen-pal service. Sponsors the *Sociedad Honoraria Hispana* and National Spanish Examinations for high school students.

American Council on the Teaching of Foreign Languages (ACTFL)
579 Broadway
Hastings-on-Hudson, NY 10706

For individuals interested in the teaching of classical and modern foreign languages in schools throughout America. Included in the council are state, regional, and national organizations of foreign-language teachers and supervisors from all school levels. ACTFL operates a center that offers teachers inexpensive classroom and professional materials.

Association of Hispanic Artists
200 E. 87th Street
New York, NY 10028

Asociación Nacional de Grupos Folklóricos
1633 Clark
Detroit, MI 48209

An organization that welcomes groups or individuals interested in learning folk dances of Latin American countries. Dance, costumes, and culture are promoted. Has an annual convention.

Association of Teachers of Latin American Studies (ATLAS)
252-58 63rd Avenue
Little Neck, NY 11362

For educators, graduate students, and others interested in promoting teaching about Latin America in U.S. schools. Conducts teacher-training workshops, seminars, and lectures; sponsors low-cost flights to Latin America. Has conducted three Fulbright programs for the U.S. Department of Education in Latin America. Maintains 600-volume library.

Bilingual Teachers Association
619 W. Clearfield Street
Philadelphia, PA 19140

Casa Aztlán
1831 S. Racine
Chicago, IL 60608

Chicago Office of Fine Arts
Cultural Center
78 E. Washington Street
Chicago, IL 60602

Club de las Américas
1724 N. Troy Street
Apt. 775
Arlington, VA 22201

For persons interested in studying the Spanish language and knowing more about the countries of Latin America and the Iberian peninsula. Offers courses on a variety of topics in Spanish.

Conference on Latin American History
Center for Latin American Studies
San Diego State University
San Diego, CA 92182

For individuals and groups with an interest in the history and civilization of Latin American countries. Holds annual competitions for books and articles on Latin American history and awards several prizes for historical publications.

Council of Spanish-Speaking Organizations (El Concilio)
705–709 N. Franklin Street
Philadelphia, PA 19123

El Taller
3321 W. Paulina
Chicago, IL 60647

Georgetown University Bilingual Education Service Center
Suite 376
D.C. Transit Building
3520 Prospect Street, N.W.
Washington, D.C. 20007

Hispanic American Organization
625 Chew Street, 2nd Floor
Allentown, PA 18102

Hispanic Center
227 N. 4th Street
Reading, PA 19601

Illinois Arts Council
100 W. Randolph Street
Suite 10
Chicago, IL 60601

Instituto Internacional de Literatura Iberoamericana
1312 C.L.
University of Pittsburgh
Pittsburgh, PA 15260

This organization seeks to promote the study of literature and to strengthen cultural relations between the peoples of North and South America. The institute publishes the works of major Latin American authors in the original language.

Inter-American Council for Education, Science and Culture (CIECC)
1889 F Street, N.W.
Washington, D.C. 20006

Latin American Community Center
1200 W. 7th Street
Wilmington, DE 19805

Latin American Studies Association (LASA)
University of Texas
Austin, TX 78712

For persons and institutions with scholarly interests in Latin America.

Latino Institute
53 W. Jackson Boulevard
Chicago, IL 60604

Mexican Fine Arts Center
P.O. Box 5177
Chicago, IL 60680-5177

Movimiento Artístico Chicano
P.O. Box 2890
Chicago, IL 60690

National Association for Bilingual Education
1201 16th Street, N.W.
Room 405
Washington, D.C. 20036

For educators, administrators, interested lay people, and students. It aims at promoting and publicizing bilingual education in the United States. This organization makes use of publications, speakers, consultants, meetings, and the mass media to foster public recognition of excellence in bilingual instruction.

Puerto Rican Arts and Cultural Center
971 Clifford Avenue
Rochester, NY 14621

Society of Hispanic Professional Engineers (SHPE)
Midwest Regional Chicago Chapter
13177 S. Brainard Avenue
Chicago, IL 60633

The major goal of SHPE is the betterment of the Hispanic community through professional development. This organization features a wide range of activities and services. Current projects include: career orientation, promotion of Hispanics within the professions, community activities, and public relations.

Spanish-American Civic Association
545 Pershing Street
Lancaster, PA 17602

Spanish Information Center
Language Department
Chicago Public Library
(312) 269-2950

This is a telephone service only.

2. *Broadcasts in Spanish*

The following is a list of radio stations (arranged by state) that broadcast 50 percent or more of their time in Spanish. Most of the stations listed broadcast full-time in Spanish. Programs include music from Latin America, news, interviews, public-service announcements, speeches, book reviews, and sports.

Arizona

KIFN-AM (860 KHz)
147 E. Garfield
Phoenix, AZ 85001

KPHX-AM (1480 KHz)
1975 S. Central Avenue
Phoenix, AZ 85004

California

KTNQ-AM (1020 KHz)
5724 Hollywood Boulevard
Los Angeles, CA 90028

KWKW-AM (1300 KHz)
6777 Hollywood Boulevard
Hollywood, CA 90028

KBRG-FM (105.3 MHz)
1355 Market Street
San Francisco, CA 94103

KNTA-AM (1430 KHz)
P.O. Box 6528
San Jose, CA 95150

KBBF-FM (89.1 MHz)
P.O. Box 7189
Santa Rosa, CA 95401

Colorado

KBNO-AM (1220 KHz)
1601 W. Jewell Avenue
Denver, CO 80223

KAPI-AM (690 KHz)
2829 Lowell Boulevard
Pueblo, CO 81003

Connecticut

WLVH-FM (93.7 MHz)
18 Asylum Street
Hartford, CT 06103

Florida

WNJK-AM (1220 KHz)
1200 Central Avenue
Kissimmee, FL 32741

WCMQ-AM (1220 KHz)
1411 Coral Way
Miami, FL 33145

WHTT-AM (1260 KHz)
P.O. Box 450550
Miami, FL 33145

WRHC-AM *(1550 KHz)*
2260 S.W. 8th Street
Miami, FL 33135

Illinois

WCRW-AM *(1240 KHz)*
2756 Pine Grove Avenue
Chicago, IL 60614

WEDC-AM *(1240 KHz)*
5475 N. Milwaukee Avenue
Chicago, IL 60630

WOJO-FM *(105 MHz)*
2425 Main Street
Evanston, IL 60202

WOPA-AM *(1490 KHz)*
408 S. Oak Park Avenue
Oak Park, IL 60302

Louisiana

KGLA-AM *(1540 KHz)*
P.O. Box 428
Marrero, LA 70072

Maryland

WMDO-AM *(1540 KHz)*
2647 University Boulevard
Wheaton, MD 20902

New Jersey

WREY-AM *(1440 KHz)*
P.O. Box 1440
South Vineland, NJ 08360

New Mexico

KABQ-AM *(1350 KHz)*
P.O. Box 4486
Albuquerque, NM 87106

KNMX-AM *(540 KHz)*
615 Lincoln Avenue
Las Vegas, NM 87701

New York

WADO-AM *(1280 KHz)*
666 3rd Avenue
New York, NY 10017

WJIT-AM *(1480 KHz)*
655 Madison Avenue
New York, NY 10021

Texas

KMXX-FM *(102.3 MHz)*
121 E. 8th Street
Austin, TX 78701

KCCT-AM *(1150 KHz)*
701 Benys
Corpus Christi, TX 78405

KAMA-AM *(1060 KHz)*
4150 Pinnacle Street
El Paso, TX 79902

KEYH-AM *(950 KHz)*
3130 Southwest Freeway
Houston, TX 77098

KCOR-AM *(1350 KHz)*
1115 W. Martin
San Antonio, TX 78207

The following is a list of television stations (arranged by state) that broadcast 50 percent or more of their time in Spanish. Most of the stations listed broadcast full-time in Spanish. The programs include educational programs, sports, political debates, drama, movies, children's programs, public-service announcements, editorials, and cultural programs.

Arizona

KTVW-TV (Channel 33)
3019 E. Southern
Phoenix, AZ 85040

California

KBSC-TV (Channel 52)
1139 Grand Central Avenue
Glendale, CA 91201

KMEX-TV (Channel 34)
5420 Melrose Avenue
Hollywood, CA 90038

KDTV (Channel 14)
2200 Palou Avenue
San Francisco, CA 94124

Florida

WLTV (Channel 23)
2525 S.W. 3rd Avenue, No. 412
Miami, FL 33129

Illinois

WCIU-TV (Channel 26)
141 W. Jackson Boulevard
Chicago, IL 60604

WSNS-TV (Channel 44)
430 W. Grant Place
Chicago, IL 60614

New Jersey

WNJU-TV (Channel 47)
1020 Broad Street
Newark, NJ 07102

WXTV (Channel 41)
24 Meadowland Parkway
Secaucus, NJ 07094

Texas

KORO-TV (Channel 28)
102 N. Mesquite
Corpus Christi, TX 78401

KWEX-TV (Channel 41)
P.O. Box 9225
San Antonio, TX 78204

3. *Hispanic-oriented Publications*

The following are magazines distributed nationally in high Hispanic population areas.

Buenhogar
De Armas Publications
535 5th Avenue
New York, NY 10017

Semi-monthly publication in Spanish with articles on home decoration
and cooking.

Geomundo
De Armas Publications
535 5th Avenue
New York, NY 10017

Bimonthly publication in Spanish with articles of general interest, news
about Latin America, recipes, puzzles, etc.

Gráfica
Orbe Publications
705 N. Windsor Boulevard
Hollywood, CA 90029

Bimonthly publication in Spanish with articles about the family.

Hispanic Business
Hispanic Business Publications
360 S. Hope Avenue
Suite 100 C
Santa Barbara, CA 93105

Monthly publication in English with professional articles on business.

Hispanic Engineer
Subscription Dept.
280 S. Sadler Avenue
Los Angeles, CA 90022

A monthly publication in Spanish and English devoted to science and
technology. A good source of information for students wishing to pursue
a career in a technical field.

Hispanic USA
161 W. Harrison Street
Chicago, IL 60605

A monthly publication in English that presents national news and issues affecting the Hispanic community.

Ideas
De Armas Publications
535 5th Avenue
New York, NY 10017

Monthly publication in Spanish with articles of general interest.

Mecánica Popular
De Armas Publications
535 5th Avenue
New York, NY 10017

Monthly publication in Spanish with articles on technical subjects. Good source for developing a larger vocabulary in that area.

National Council of La Raza
20 F Street, N.W.
Washington, D.C. 20001

Bilingual, bimonthly publication with information about professional and community organizations.

Nuestro
Nuestro Publications, Inc.
461 Park Avenue, S.
New York, NY 10016

Monthly, bilingual (90% English) publication with articles on all aspects of Latin America—customs, cities, government, history, art, legends, as well as articles on contributions made by great Hispanic people. Good source of research information.

Quinto Lingo
Rodale Press, Inc.
33 E. Minor Street
Emmaus, PA 18049

Monthly publication with stories and news items in five languages (German, French, Spanish, Italian, Russian).

Temas
1650 Broadway
New York, NY 10019

Monthly publication in Spanish with articles about the family.

Vanidades
De Armas Publications
535 5th Avenue
New York, NY 10017

Biweekly Spanish-language publication with articles on Latin America. It includes recipes, decoration ideas, travel ideas, etc.

4. Newspapers

The following are newspapers distributed nationally in high Hispanic population areas.

Diario Las Américas
2900 N.W. 39th Street
Miami, FL 33142

Daily newspaper in Spanish with news and articles of interest to high school students.

El Diario–La Prensa
181 Hudson Street
New York, NY 10013

Daily newspaper in Spanish, with news, interviews, and articles of interest to the Hispanic community.

La Opinión
1436 S. Main Street
Los Angeles, CA 90015

Daily Spanish-language newspaper of general interest and content, covering local, national, and international news.

Laredo News
P.O. Box 2129
Laredo, TX 78041

Spanish-English daily circulation.

Laredo Times
P.O. Box 2129
Laredo, TX 78041

Spanish- and English-language daily.

Noticias de Este Mundo
401 5th Avenue
New York, NY 10016

Daily newspaper in Spanish. It includes international news and events of interest to advanced high school students.

5. Pen Pals

Ambassadors of Friendship
4300 Lennox Drive
Miami, FL 33133

Ages 13 to 18.

American Pen Pals
701 N. 6th Street
Herrin, IL 62948

High school students.

Children's Plea for Peace
World Affairs Center
University of Minnesota
Minneapolis, MN 55455

Ages 10 to 18, also teacher-to-teacher correspondence.

Dyer's Pen-Pal Service Organization
R.F.D. 3
Sequin, TX 78155

Ages 12 to 16.

International Friendship League
22 Batterymarch Street
Boston, MA 02109

An international correspondence organization that matches Americans of all ages with pen pals in 139 foreign locales. Sponsors a speakers bureau for junior high schools, high schools, colleges, and universities. Maintains a small library with books on foreign countries. Sponsors competitions and research programs.

League of Friendship, Inc.
P.O. Box 509
Mount Vernon, OH 43050

Ages 12 to 25.

Letters Abroad, Inc.
209 E. 56th Street
New York, NY 10022

Ages 15 and over.

Letter Exchange Program
People-to-People, Inc.
2401 Grand Avenue
Kansas City, MO 64108

Ages 14 and over.

Student Letter Exchange
910 4th Street, S.E.
Austin, TX 55912

The goal of this organization is to build international goodwill through pen-pal correspondence between young people between the ages of 10 and 19 in the U.S. and 50 other countries. A dollar is charged for every pen-pal name received.

Student Letter Exchange
R.F.D. 4
Waseca, MN 56093

Ages 10 to 19.

The Voicepondence Club
P.O. Box 14492
Long Beach, CA 90814

Correspondence by tape (four per year); includes annual directory of members and a quarterly publication.

World Pen Pals
University of Minnesota
2001 Riverside Avenue
Minneapolis, MN 55404

Ages 12 to 20 and teacher-to-teacher program.

World Tape Pals, Inc.
P.O. Box 9211
Dallas, TX 75216

Correspondence by tape.

Worldwide Tapetalk
35, The Gardens
West Harrow
Middlesex HA1 4HE
England

For individuals interested in forming worldwide friendships through verbal communication. Uses the tape recorder to promote a better understanding between people of all nations. Conducts roundtable discussion groups. Offers tape/slide presentations, as well as movies with commentaries. Maintains a library of tapes including music and documentaries. Publishes *Directory of Tape Stations* (3 issues a year) and *Sound Advice* (3 isssues a year). Also publishes *Tips for Tapepondents.*

Youth of All Nations, Inc.
16 St. Luke's Place
New York, NY 10014

Teenagers and young adults.

6. *Study Programs Abroad*

Classrooms Abroad
P.O. Box 4171
University Station
Minneapolis, MN 55414

Summer study session, followed by a two-week trip. Application form by request.

Foreign Study League
164 E. 3900, S.
Salt Lake City, UT 84107

Summer study sessions in Spanish-speaking countries for students with at least a B-average; no Spanish-language requirement.

International School Service
554 5th Avenue
New York, NY 10017

Study abroad.

International Youth Academies
317 14th Avenue, S.E.
Minneapolis, MN 55414

High school and pre-college programs. Departure from and return to Chicago.

National Committee for Students Abroad (NCSA)
339 Walnut Street
Philadelphia, PA 19106

Student programs and job opportunities abroad.

UNESCO Publications Center
317 E. 34th Street
New York, NY 10016

Vacations abroad.

U.S. National Student Association
265 Madison Avenue
New York, NY 10016

Work, study, and travel programs; publishes a handbook of student travel; provides information about international student I.D. cards and youth hostels.

World Academy
Gwynne Building
Sixth and Main Streets
P.O. Box 1847
Cincinnati, OH 45202

Offers a wide choice of accredited foreign-study programs for high school students in summer. Send for group adviser's brochure and student catalogue.

Airlines often have special rates for groups of 15 or more when traveling overseas. Prices vary according to size of group and duration of trip.

7. Exchange-Student Programs

American Field Service (AFS)
313 E. 43rd Street
New York, NY 10017

International Christian Youth Exchange
74 Trinity Place
New York, NY 10006

United States Catholic Conference
1312 Massachusetts Avenue, N.W.
Washington, D.C. 20005

The three organizations listed above sponsor summer and school-year programs for members of high school, church, or other groups. High school students from the United States are placed with families in a foreign country; high school students from foreign countries live with families in the United States.

8. Hispanic Import Items

Amigo Country
541 Atlantic Avenue
Brooklyn, NY 11217

Direct importers of furniture and handicrafts.

Casa Esteiro Spanish-Latin American Products
2719 W. Division Street
Chicago, IL 60622

Imported foods from Latin American countries.

Casa de Pancho Import Items
1349 Orange Avenue
Coronado, CA 92118

Mexican craft items, excellent for gifts.

Cielito Lindo Mexican Imports
2455 Juan Street
San Diego, CA 92110

Mexican craft items, gifts, records, books, and souvenirs.

El Mundo Supermarket
42–16 Junction Boulevard
Flushing, NY 11368

Hispanic food, import items, souvenirs, gift items, records, books.

El Rey Deli
5039 Shawlime
San Diego, CA 92111

Homemade Mexican delicacies.

El Yunque Spanish-American Store, Ltd.
43–21 Beach Channel Drive
Far Rockaway, NY 11691

Complete line of Hispanic products.

Goya Foods, Inc.
100 Seaview Drive
Secaucus, NY 07094

Importers of Latin American and Spanish food products.

Iberia Foods, Inc.
60 Snediker Avenue
Brooklyn, NY 11207

Spanish and Latin American food products.

La Flor de Cuba
49–02 43rd Avenue
Flushing, NY 11377
Cuban food, delicacies, gifts, records, books.

La Preferida, Inc. of Chicago
3400 W. 35th Street
Chicago, IL 60632

Fresh fruits and vegetables (as well as frozen), canned foods, meats, fish, and cheese from Latin America and the Caribbean.

La Preferida, Inc. of New York
945 Close Avenue
Bronx, NY 10473

Importers of a complete line of Latin American foods.

Spanish Resources and Activities

Mexican Folk Arts
2433 N. Clark Street
Chicago, IL 60614

Mexican craft items.

The Mexico Shop
2723 San Diego Avenue
San Diego, CA 92110

Sells all types of ingredients to prepare a homemade Mexican dish and offers Mexican import items.

Todo Imports, Ltd.
2113 Kerrigan Avenue
Union City, NJ 07087

Importers of Latin American products, gifts, records, and periodicals.

Toro Imports Co.
412 N. Orleans
Chicago, IL 60610

Fur rugs and decorative accessories from Latin America.

Zala Mexican Deli and Tortilla Factory
656 Mafat Court
Chula Vista, CA 92010

Deli and food products.

9. Fund-raising Items

Fuller Fund Raising
P.O. Box 18324
Louisville, KY 40218

Tom-Wat, Inc.
765 Fairfield Avenue
Bridgeport, CT 06601

10. *Latin American and Caribbean Recipe Books*

The following books are good sources of recipes for club festivities.

Cocine a Gusto
by Carmen Ginorio and Carmen Q. Mercado
Editorial Universidad de Puerto Rico
San Juan, Puerto Rico, 1983

Cocina con Usted
by Ana Dolores Goméz de Dumois
Cultural Puertorriqueña, Inc.
San Juan, Puerto Rico, 1983

Cocina General
by Margarita de la Fuente
Editores Mexicanos Unidos, SA
Mexico City, Mexico, 1982

Cocina Mexicana
by Virginia Ramos Espinosa
Editorial Diana
Mexico City, Mexico, 1983

Puerto Rican Cookery
by Carmen Aboy Valldejuli
Pelican Publishing Company
Dredna, Louisiana, 1984

210 Recetas de Cocina Internacional
by Virginia Ramos Espinosa
Editorial Diana
Mexico City, Mexico, 1979

A bookstore where all these cookbooks may be ordered is:
Yuquiyu Publications
2546 W. Division Street
Chicago, IL 60622

NTC SPANISH TEXTS AND MATERIALS

Computer Software
Basic Vocabulary Builder on Computer
Amigo: Vocabulary Software

**Videocassette, Activity Book,
and Instructor's Manual**
VideoPasaporte Español

Graded Readers
Diálogos simpáticos
Cuentitos simpáticos
Cuentos simpáticos
Beginner's Spanish Reader
Easy Spanish Reader

Workbooks
Así escribimos
Ya escribimos
¡A escribir!
Composiciones ilustradas
Spanish Verb Drills

Exploratory Language Books
Spanish for Beginners
Let's Learn Spanish Picture Dictionary
Spanish Picture Dictionary
Getting Started in Spanish
Just Enough Spanish

Conversation Books
¡Empecemos a charlar!
Basic Spanish Conversation
Everyday Conversations in Spanish

Manual and Audiocassette
How to Pronounce Spanish Correctly

**Text and Audiocassette Learning
Packages**
Just Listen 'n Learn Spanish
Just Listen 'n Learn Spanish Plus
Practice and Improve Your Spanish
Practice and Improve Your Spanish
 Plus

High-Interest Readers
Sr. Pepino Series
 La momia desaparece
 La casa embrujada
 El secuestro

Journeys to Adventure Series
 Un verano misterioso
 La herencia
 El ojo de agua
 El enredo
 El jaguar curioso

Humor in Spanish and English
Spanish à la Cartoon

Puzzle and Word Game Books
Easy Spanish Crossword Puzzles
Easy Spanish Word Games & Puzzles
Easy Spanish Vocabulary Puzzles

Transparencies
Everyday Situations in Spanish

Black-line Masters
Spanish Verbs and Vocabulary Bingo Games
Spanish Crossword Puzzles
Spanish Culture Puzzles
Spanish Word Games
Spanish Vocabulary Puzzles

Handbooks and Reference Books
Complete Handbook of Spanish Verbs
Spanish Verbs and Essentials of Grammar
Nice 'n Easy Spanish Grammar
Tratado de ortografía razonada
Redacte mejor comercialmente
Guide to Correspondence in Spanish
Guide to Spanish Idioms

Dictionaries
Vox Modern Spanish and English Dictionary
Vox New College Spanish and English Dictionary
Vox Compact Spanish and English Dictionary
Vox Everyday Spanish and English Dictionary
Vox Traveler's Spanish and English Dictionary
Vox Super-Mini Spanish and English Dictionary
Cervantes-Walls Spanish and English Dictionary

For further information or a current catalog, write:
National Textbook Company
a division of *NTC Publishing Group*
4255 West Touhy Avenue
Lincolnwood, Illinois 60646-1975 U.S.A.